SLAM!

Performance Poetry from the Underrepresented

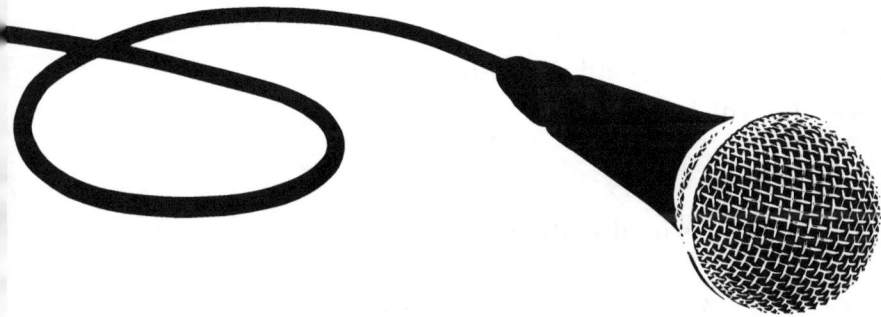

KINSMAN AVENUE PUBLISHING, INC.
www.kinsmanquarterly.org

© 2024 Kinsman Avenue Publishing, Inc.

Registered with the U.S. Library of Congress
Library of Congress Control Number: 2024924024

Printed in the United States of America

SLAM! Performance Poetry from
the Underrepresented

ISBN: 978-1-962121-13-2   Paperback
ISBN: 978-1-962121-14-9   eBook format

Book Design by Summer Greigh

Creative Editor: Monique Franz
Co-Editors: Akin Jeje and Odette Cortés
Supporting edits: Sophia Obianamma Ofuokwu and
Radiyah Nouman
Submissions Manager: Yolanda Simpson
Submissions Intern: Anthony Charles

Contributing authors in alphabetical order:

Aanika Pfister, Ade Anita Johnson, Akin Jeje, Amy-Lenna Bryce, Angela Gyurko, Brother Tshepang, Carmen dela Cruz, Courtney Seymour, Diego Alejandro Arias, Jonathan Chibuike Ukah, Jon Jon Stefan, Karen Lynette Jones, Kathy Gregg, Libby Young, Lola–La Revolution–Rosario, Lucas Rivera, Lucy Collins, Mark Havlik, Monique Franz, Patricia Knight Meyer, Ryan Files, Tonnie MAC, Trish Broome, Walt Shulits, Yolanda Simpson

SLAM!

Performance Poetry from the Underrepresented

Edited by Monique Franz
Co-Editors: Akin Jeje and Odette Cortés
Cover Design: Summer Greigh

Dedicated to those who explore truth in verse.

Monique's Note

In 1984, a Chicago construction worker, Marc Smith, laid the foundation for slam poetry. Driven by a desire to bring poetry to the stage in a way that was fun, competitive, and engaging, he revolutionized the art form, turning it into a powerful performative expression. The culture of slam includes raw, unapologetic, and radical verse, tackling themes like social justice, identity, love, and trauma—giving voice to both personal and societal struggles. This collection of poetry perfectly captures that culture.

I remember attending my first poetry slam in Hong Kong, hosted by Peel Street Poetry under the direction of Nashua Gallagher, Henrik Hoeg, and Akin Jeje. I was captivated by the boldness of the poets, dropping truth bombs in verse and going off the rails of political correctness. That was new to me. I wrote solemn songs and poetry that hid my rage in images of nature, like giving a pill to a child under a spoonful of ice cream. I would beat around the bush of truth—tucking harsh realities among picturesque verbiage. Not these poets I witnessed onstage. They were brutally honest, sometimes offensive, using their words like weapons to tear down, uproot, and knock out. Such honesty is what you will find here within these pages.

In 2024, Kinsman Quarterly reached out to poets worldwide to find the most creative works that embodied the essence of slam poetry—raw, rhythmic, hard-hitting, and competitive. The competition was overseen by KQ's vice president, Yolanda Simpson, a recording Hip-Hop artist who knows all about delivering gut–punching bars. Yolanda contributed many of her own verses to this collection, alongside the top winners: Brother Tshepang from South Africa, Carmen dela Cruz from Washington State, Jonathan Chibuike Ukah of the UK, and Lola "La Revolution" Rosario from Puerto Rico, along with many other gifted poets from around the world, including yours truly.

– Monique Franz, *Senior Editor*

A
virgin page
longing for the
fertilization of a
pen to birth truth
or to birth lies; to
craft mysteries or
or to draw guides;
to create worlds of
new colors or trees
in random shades; to
articulate passionate
love made. Ink that
reveals and scolds
those loved & those
loathed, those held
and hurt; to dig up
bones, or to shovel
some dirt. The pen
brings to life my
dreams & prayers;   &
fears & nightmares;   &
it resurrects the dead;   &
any words left unsaid;   &
any anger or envy; joy   &
lust; hope, peace, trust,   &
regrets; there's tension   &
quests for redemption   &
keen description   to
remember of   one's
eyes, hair, or   teeth;
to capture   the
memory   of
that which
captured
me.

Virgin Page
Monique Franz

Truth Serum: Poetic Prophets

Image: Distorted and Discovered

The Heart: Love and War

Mental Health: Surrender or Conquer

Home: Heritage and Pride

Our Forefathers: Sins and Wins

Justice: The Cry of the Land

Resilience: Past and Present

BROTHER TSHEPANG
Grand Prize Winner
"Ghetto Gospels"

Brother Tshepang Mugandi, grand prize winner of the Kinsman Poetry Slam, is a South African poet, programmer, musician, translator, and academic from Vosloorus, Johannesburg. His passion for poetry began at age 9, leading him to release works across audio, video, and written formats. Tshepang's poetry, rich in philosophy, theology, history, and social justice, is written in several languages, including English, Afrikaans, isiZulu, isiXhosa, and Sesotho. Educated at Laerskool Van Dyk and Sunward Park High School, he excelled in writing and performing poetry and music in multiple languages. Tshepang is currently pursuing a certificate in Full Stack Development with Free Code Camp, aiming to contribute to Africa's 4th Industrial Revolution. His award-winning poetry collection, Ghetto Gospels, confronts social injustices in South Africa while offering hope for divine justice and redemption.

1

CARMEN DELA CRUZ
1st Runner-Up
"Damn the Light-Skinned Lottery"

Carmen dela Cruz, the 1st Runner-Up in the 2024 Kinsman Poetry Slam, is a Black Southern writer with an MFA in Creative Writing from Chatham University. Now living in Spokane, Washington, she is pursuing a Doctorate in Leadership Studies at Gonzaga University. Her poem "The Silent Fight" was published in *The Fourth River's Black Visions: A Jeffery 'Boosie' Bolden Anthology* (Summer 2022), and her essay "Selma: An Exploration of the Womanist Lens and the Servant-Leader" was featured in the *International Journal of Servant-Leadership* (2020) before being selected for *Servant Leadership, Feminism, and Gender Well-Being* (SUNY Press, 2022). Her recent poems, "Under the Surface" and "Forgive Me," appeared in the November 2023 issue of the *International Journal of Servant-Leadership.* Carmen's work focuses on social justice, leadership, and womanism, using her voice to amplify marginalized communities and explore the intricate facets of Black identity in America.

JONATHAN CHIBUIKE UKAH
2nd Runner Up
"I Blame My Ancestors"

Jonathan Chibuike Ukah is a Pushcart-nominated poet from the United Kingdom. His work has appeared in *Clockhouse, Atticus Review, Kinsman Quarterly, Silk Road, The Pierian*, and other literary outlets. In 2023, he won the prestigious Alexander Pope Poetry Award and was shortlisted for the Minds Shine Bright Poetry Prize in 2024. Jonathan's poetry delves into themes of identity, heritage, and human experience, earning him recognition on both national and international platforms.

LOLA ROSARIO
3rd Runner Up
"This Soil in My Blood"

Lola—La Revolution—Rosario is an Afro-Indigenous Boricua spoken word poet, freelance journalist, and translator from New York City. Her work centers on celebrating Puerto Rican heritage, focusing on Indigenous Taíno, Iñeri, and African ancestry. She writes about cultural pride, colonization, diaspora identity, and racism. Her debut poetry collection, *Daughter de Borikén* (Editorial Pulpo), releases in August 2024. Her poems have appeared in *The Acentos Review, La Libreta.online, Thin Air Magazine*, and *Hound Magazine*. Lola's social justice journalism is featured in outlets like *NACLA, Hip Latina*, and *Latina Media*. She now resides in Loíza, Puerto Rico.

Top Finalists (in ABC order)

ADE ANITA JOHNSON
"Resistance, Resilience, and Resurrection"

Ade Anita Johnson is a spoken word artist, celebrated for her "modern dance on the page" style. She is the author of *Resistance, Resilience, and Resurrection—A Three Poem Collection* and the 2023 chapbook *Moving in Twilight—Searching in the Dark*. Ade's work explores themes of love, identity, justice, and the divine, drawing inspiration from her deep connection to nature and heritage. She founded *Colors of Light—Black People Write*, a global online community. In addition to writing, Ade is a speaker, coach, certified transformational leader, and meditation teacher. She holds a BA in English and Theatre from Mount Holyoke College and is a member of the 5th Woman Poetry Collective and Knoxville Writer's Guild. Ade resides in Knoxville, TN.

AMY-LENNA BRYCE
"The Rage"

Amy-Lenna Bryce, a queer poet from Hertfordshire, UK, was a finalist in the 2024 Kinsman Poetry Slam. Her poetry collection, *The Rage*, explores themes of inner turmoil, body image, mental health, and trauma, drawing from deeply personal experiences. Her work has appeared in *Ink and Marrow Lit* (Issue 6), and she has a poem forthcoming in an anthology by Gnashing Teeth Publishing. Amy-Lenna's evocative writing captures the rawness of emotional struggles, offering a voice to those with similar experiences. Follow her on Instagram @amylennabryce.

DIEGO ALEJANDRO ARIAS
"We A-OK, USA"

Diego Alejandro Arias is a Colombian-American writer, diplomat, lawyer, and civil rights activist who has called New Jersey home for over three decades. Originally from Medellín, Colombia, Diego's writing explores themes of identity, justice, and cultural heritage. His work has been published in *Another Chicago Magazine, Somos En Escrito, The Arlington Literary Journal, Acentos Review, Action, Spectacle*, and more. With a deep commitment to civil rights and social justice, his writing reflects his dedication to amplifying marginalized voices. Connect with Diego at realdiegoarias.com.

LUCAS RIVERA
"Not About the Color of Our Skin"

Lucas Rivera is an Afro-Puerto Rican artist whose work spans music, dance, painting, and poetry, all reflecting his rich cultural heritage. Born and raised in North Philadelphia, he honed his artistic voice through the vibrant community of Taller Puertorriqueño. Rivera has captivated audiences in Philadelphia, New York, Miami, and Puerto Rico, using his performances and exhibitions to explore the depth of his Afro-Rican identity. He is the Founder and CEO of Sakul Creative, LLC, a boutique agency specializing in cultural arts consulting, event strategy, and program development.

MARK HAVLIK
"Two into One into None"

Mark Havlik's work has appeared in Trajectory, *The Hungry Chimera, Anomaly, Flying South, The Blue Mountain Review, Star 82 Review, Kaleidoscope, Chaleur Magazine, Passing Through, South Florida Arts Journal, Santa Fe Writers Project Literary Journal,* and *Washington The Magazine.* A finalist in the 2024 Kinsman Poetry Slam, his poem "Two into One into None" compellingly portrays a man's inner turmoil and descent into self-destruction. Mark's writing addresses themes of identity, struggle, and transformation, offering readers profound insight into the human experience.

TRISH BROOME
"Sibling Sobriety"

Trish Broome is a half-Korean writer and poet from Newport News, Virginia. She holds a B.A. from Longwood College and an M.A. from Loyola University Maryland. Her work has appeared in *You Might Need to Hear This, Half and One, Cure Today,* and the upcoming AMPLIFY issue of *Yellow Arrow Vignette.* She is also a contributor to *A Letter to My Mom.* Trish lives in Maryland with her husband, daughter, and two rescue dogs. When not working at the local library, she enjoys 90s hip hop and perfecting her kimchi recipe. Follow her on Instagram @trishb. poetry or visit trishbroome.com.

Honorable Mentions (in ABC order)

AANIKA PFISTER
"Questions for the State of Iowa"

Aanika Pfister is a slam poet and writer, as well as a proud alumna of Drake University. Her multicultural heritage and Chicago roots deeply influence her work, which centers on the representation of minority communities, particularly Black Americans. Her poetry has been featured in *Contratiempo*, and she has been commissioned by Illinois Humanities. Aanika also contributed to the creation of *Sacrifice State: Iowa Voices on Environment & Justice*. Currently, she is applying to graduate programs while researching and writing about historically overlooked Black women. In her spare time, you might catch her on the "L," at her local comic book shop, or wrangling her three cats—Hugo, William, and Kai.

ANGELA GYURKO
"Do You Have a Plan?"

Angela Gyurko, longlister of the 2024 Kinsman Poetry Slam, pursued various careers before earning her MFA from Goddard College in 2019. Her passion for playwriting emerged along with her desire to be a novelist, leading several of her poetic works to be staged. Recent global conflicts reignited her poetic voice, resulting in her first long-form poem since the 1990s. When not writing, Angela is a dedicated activist for voting rights and healthcare reform.

COURTNEY SEYMOUR
"It Comes with the Territory"

Courtney Seymour holds a B.S. in Biology from Union College and an M.L.S. in Library Science, along with an M.A. in English, from the State University of New York at Albany. She is a librarian, instructor of research and persuasion at Southern New Hampshire University, domestic violence advocate, and mother. A New England transplant, Courtney's poetry has been published in *Whispered Words: A Writer Shed Press Poetry Project*, *TPT Magazine*, and *The Elevation Review*. Her work reflects her commitment to education, advocacy, and creative expression.

KAREN LYNETTE JONES
"Purple Poet Tree"

Karen Lynette Jones, born in Charlotte, North Carolina, is a mother to her son, Tahj. She holds a Bachelor of Science in Criminal Justice from Gardner-Webb University and an Associate of Science in Paralegal Technology from Central Piedmont College. Karen is currently developing a book inspired by her 3D animation project, *Dragon Stew*. In 2024, she received an honorable mention in the Kinsman Poetry Slam for her work. Her poetry collection, *Purple Poet Tree*, discusses themes of culture, resilience, and pride, reflecting her deep commitment to storytelling and creative expression.

KATHY GREGG
"Iya, the Magic Lady"

Kathy Gregg is a South Carolina-based writer who has been crafting stories and poetry since the age of 10. Her work is deeply influenced by her multicultural heritage, spirituality, and the supernatural. Poetry, in particular, has always been her greatest passion, stirring her soul and fueling her creativity. Her poem "Iya, the Magic Lady," a tribute to her great-grandmother, received an honorable mention at the 2024 Kinsman Poetry Slam. Kathy's writing delves into the mystical and the divine, blending her rich cultural background with themes of spirituality and the unseen.

LIBBY YOUNG
"Bodies"

Libby Young is a fantasy writer based in Scotland, where she lives with her partner and two cats. Currently navigating the challenging world of traditional publishing with two completed novels, she is also hard at work on her third. Her short story, "The Catch," has been featured on the *Tales to Terrify* podcast. While Libby may joke about having the social media skills of a grandmother, she is passionate about raising awareness for those suffering from endometriosis, adenomyosis, PCOS, and other underfunded and under-researched gynecologic conditions. She advocates for better treatment and support for those affected by these often overlooked issues.

LUCY COLLINS
"The Truth"

Lucy Collins is a blogger at Elsie LMC, living in Ireland, where she channels her love for writing poetry and short stories as a means of escapism. Her poem "The Truth" marked her debut publication, offering a raw exploration of her past and delivering the important message that it's okay not to be okay. While this is her first time being published, Lucy is determined to continue sharing her voice through future publications. Her writing, both on her blog and in her creative works, fosters a deep connection with readers seeking authenticity and emotional release.

PATRICIA KNIGHT MEYER
"Bi-Bedtime Stories"

Patricia Knight Meyer splits her time between the Texas Hill Country and her tiny house in New Orleans. Patricia writes prose, essays, short stories, book reviews, magazine articles, and poetry, while also maintaining her blog, *My Adopted Life*, and contributing to *Medium*. A passionate advocate for feminist causes, reproductive rights, and adoption reform, her writing reflects her commitment to these important issues. Connect with her on social media @myadoptedlife and @somebodys__baby.

RYAN FILES
"Circuitous Revolution"

Ryan Files is an educator, writer, editor, and poet who serves as a teaching artist at Arizona State University's Piper Center, focusing on creative writing. In 2023, he was a semifinalist in the Arizona spoken word state competition and a finalist in the Writer's Digest National Poetry Competition for his poem "Harlem Noir." His work appears in anthologies from Middle West Press and Moonstone Publishing, and his book *Half Dollar Moments* is included in the Indie Arizona collection, available in libraries statewide. Connect with him at fileswrites@gmail.com for teaching, writing, or editing opportunities.

WALT SHULITS
"Uncle Sam's"

Walt Shulits, a retired bond market professional and lifelong paddling enthusiast, discovered poetry while seeking a non-sport activity that captured the same "in the moment" sensation as canoeing and kayaking. With a passion for paddling everything from sea kayaks to surf skis, he divides his time between Provence, France, and his cherished Hawaii. Walt strives to write poetry that resonates with those who find the genre incomprehensible or unappealing. His work has appeared in *Dumpster Fire, Fleas on the Dog, Gargoyle, Griffel, Piker Press,* and *Windless Dreamer.*

Team Poets (in ABC Order)

AKIN JEJE
"Captain Kangaroo"

Kinsman Quarterly's literature director Akin Jeje is a Nigerian-Canadian poet living in Hong Kong. He has published internationally, including in Canada, the United States, Singapore, Australia, the United Kingdom, and Hong Kong. His debut poetry collection, *Smoked Pearl*, was long-listed for the 2009 International Proverse Prize and published in 2010. His recent poem, "Ping Shan Heritage Trail," was featured in the *WHERE ELSE: An International Hong Kong Poetry Anthology* (April 2023). Jeje has completed another poetry manuscript, *write about here*, and is working on a novel titled *Maroon*. He is also a regular contributor to *Cha: An Asian Literary Journal*.

JON JON STEFAN
"Cogs and Wires"

Jon Jon Stefan is a published poet, sociology student, and community activist with a deep-rooted passion for supporting marginalized communities and celebrating cultural diversity. Raised in the world of foreign missions, his experiences shaped his dedication to advocacy. His poetry explores the intricacies of the human psyche and the relationships that define identity. His collection, *Repatriate*, is featured in *Black Diaspora: Tales and Poems of the Sons and Daughters of Africa*. Through his writing and activism, Stefan seeks to amplify overlooked voices and foster connections across diverse communities.

MONIQUE FRANZ
"Virgin Page"

Monique Franz, founder and senior editor of Kinsman Avenue Publishing, Inc., earned her MFA in Creative Writing from Wilkes University, where she received the prestigious Beverly Hiscox and Norris Church Mailer scholarships. A published author, playwright, and teaching artist, she has traveled to 33 countries, leading workshops for actors and educators in youth and arts programs. Her works include *The Dove Training Series* and *Legacy of a Father.* As a creative editor, she has overseen publications such as *Kinsman Quarterly Magazine, Black Diaspora: Tales and Poems from the Sons and Daughters of Africa, Native Voices, and SLAM!*

TONNIE MAC
"Final Destination"

Tonnie MAC, Kinsman Quarterly's poetry intern and Kenyan poet, channels his experiences into powerful poetry that seeks to transcend challenges and inspire change. As his family's primary breadwinner from a young age, poetry became his refuge during high school, offering hope and solace during difficult times. MAC now actively shares his poetry, competes in literary contests, and performs at various venues. He eagerly anticipates the release of his debut poetry collection, *Child Weep No More and Other Poems.* Beyond poetry, MAC is passionate about data analytics, quality assurance, and social entrepreneurship.

YOLANDA SIMPSON
"The Plan"

Yolanda Simpson, Vice President of Kinsman Avenue Publishing, Inc., plays a pivotal role in guiding *Kinsman Quarterly* and managing global contest submissions. With over 20 years of experience as a performing artist and music producer, she brings expertise in musical composition, arrangement, and production. Simpson has crafted scores for stage plays, developed music for art-based curricula, composed for television shows, and produced tracks for independent artists. Her recent work in literary arts reflects her passion for storytelling across diverse artistic platforms. With Kinsman Quarterly, she merges her love for verse and dedication to amplifying underrepresented voices in literature.

TRUTH SERUM
Poetic Prophets

Section 1

Ghetto Gospels

Brother Tshepang

A poetry collection that brings to life the tales of Johannesburg

Spirit Filled

Sirens, gun violence, and a moment
of silence, as tyrants give no compliance
to our complaints, no remorse for our restraints.
Massacres massively maintain murder rates. In the
City of Johannesburg, the city of degenerates, where the
evil is generous with genocide and chooses to abide inside...

Inside of our hearts are memories of hurt and
happiness, along with fear of what will happen next.
A nest of naivety feeds the web of lies and supplies a big
surprise. Our very eyes will despise all that we can see from the
skies until the ground. Around and round the wheel keeps spinning
as mankind is sinning. It seems like hell is winning, this is only the beginning.

Oppressive rulers drunk with power fight the
Spirit Filled. Spirits fill masses and make them a
bit surreal; how miraculous that it's so real. What is
finally being revealed shall be revered in due time. For now
we do time in the prison of our freedom, being fooled by our wisdom.
The righteous are treasonous in the heathens' kingdom. May no evil kill them.

The Echoes

Distant echoes are heard in the direction
that the air goes. The air shows how the winds go
about with spreading their wings; like a mighty bird that
is heard like the stampede of a herd. Herd mentality has turned
many into cash cows. I ask how did blue buffaloes buy our benevolence?
Violence and tyrants operate for one hundred rands in these estranged lands.

Underground movements are moving like the Gautrain
in Gauteng's epicentre. The happy centre of Joburg will now
beg but never beg to differ. If we give a perspective that goes much
deeper than the oceans, minds might be mightier than mountains as our
focus flows like fountains. Add with the amount of amounting abundance of
bandits. Broader bandwidths of frequencies frequently firmly form a pattern.

A pat on the shoulder showed a perfect place
to be backstabbed. Baghdad could never be blown like my mind.
My blind faith has made me see the truth. Lies are mostly catered to
the youth. Hence we are fed up of being fed lies while the BS fertilise. One's
futile eyes will brutalise the neuro cortex. Horror spirals like a vortex as visions
of war tanks and turns in the wheel that drives our system to enhance wisdom.

Vain

Seeing the nation bleed makes one feel
like one's efforts are in vain. Seeing the terrain
being decorated with pain exposes the true colours
of those with black hearts. Backwards is the direction we
are taking, making this journey more miserable. There's nothing
missable about our past. Vast amounts of citizens are trapped in lions' dens.

The air is more dense as the situation gets tense.
We seemingly take turns on the driver's side of victimhood
The greater good is not what is served by the neighbourhood.
So, how will we enable good when we only want to get, but never give?
We must be naive to think that this is sustainable. Say no more, for the silence
is our witness as we see how every weakness weakens the wicked on weekends.

If we can reconcile, reconsider, and recompense
our competence will strengthen our confidence. Our
continent's Achilles Heel is the hand of corruption. Our state
can barely function. I make the assumption that some things were
made to fade. The fate of every degenerate will narrate a sad song sung
by the voiceless. These voices fill voids and vortex in one's cerebral cortex.

Cesspools

Bodies become baptised in blood baths
Certain sections are cesspools with successful
results for cults, but difficult for different kinds of minds.
Mines dug graves and gave gold, platinum, uranium, and palladium
as a sum total for the total death toll. All the falls and flaws faced the floors
to ensure we endure, we enjoy and enjoin with the broken, for stories unspoken.

With emotions and feelings awoken, many are walking
like blind men, not seeing that overlooking things leads to
blindness. This is binding our minds by combining and redefining
the fine things we are finding when seeking the truth. Speaking the truth
leads to persecution and execution in a world built on lies. Missiles fly while
missing files scatter for war criminals. Subliminal messages are our response.

Once our wants are fulfilled, our needs are forgotten
and new situations are begotten. We got in this mess by
choosing to dismiss all the clues. Articles were propagated by
propaganda. With great grandeur and splendor, governments would
spend a nation's wealth and fortune and force you to obey to Marxism.
Narcissism plagues the Southern lands of the Motherland and extends its hands.

Era

I'm in my Man of God era. No
error has been clearer, because I can sense
His presence drawing nearer. We're truly in a
ruthless area, that is surrounded by demonic terror.
One day, it will get better. The Great Battle of Armageddon
is getting close. For those who chose Adonai, look to the sky.

They will wonder why we testify and verify what sounds
like a lie. They deny what those who saw with their eyes and
lost their lives, believing it is lies. Yet the lord of flies, the father of
lies make them idolise those who utter lies. We serve a God who dies and
can rise, Yeshua the Christ. He who hears our cries, gave His life as a sacrifice
for only His blood can suffice; none else could pay the price. We are His prize.

This is a difficult path to navigate. A path that
many will never get. We enter through the Narrow
Gate. We narrate at a rate that is too fast to contemplate.
This will move tectonic plates and feed hell fire. The return of
our Messiah will be a massacre, masked with the beauty of Heaven.
The day of the heathens' punishment will be a great accomplishment.

Brother Tshepang

The Plan

Yolanda Simpson

They want to sex them up,
And get them high,
Give them a gun,
And watch them die,
Fill them with liquor, pills, stacks
and watch them fly,
Then steal their souls,
And watch them die.

My heart is so broke;
my stomach is sick.
The love of money got
our sons dying, tryna get rich.
They're killing, stealing, doing everything
for the illusion of peace
they think that money brings.

And at the end of the dolla',
I hear their souls holla',
Let me outta jail.
Let me out the grave.
Let me out of hell.

Well, that was the plan—
to kill him before he became a man.
To fry his brain before he understands
that he's a king,
destined to reign, like with the Son
of the only One begotten of the Holy One,
but instead he got an idol and he got a gun,
got some money and got some tats and
some Versace on.
And they're thinking, "yeah," to themselves,
"Yo baby that's the one—that I'm tryna get like
because his pockets weigh a ton."

Yeah, his pockets may weigh a ton,
but his soul is already gone,
and the monster he becomes
as he's misleading all our sons
to the grave.
Sell Out!
Just go get the hell out
our face.
Your images of black is a disgrace.
And our chase
for paper is a chase for vapors.

We're paying for it now and
gon' be paying for it later.
And later—it always comes.
Yeah later, it always comes.
And somebody should tell our sons,
that—that later, it always comes.

They want to sex them up,
And get them high,
Give them a gun,
And watch them die,
Fill them with liquor, pills, stacks
and watch them fly,
Then steal their souls,
And watch them die.

I'm ashamed of sometimes
of how we look on the street.
We're not perverted, drunken criminals
that's packin' that heat,
but that's the image that they put out,
so, don't you get mad at me.
Yo, when these rappers drop that garbage,
and we treat it like heat.
They be like,
"Kill my nigga," "steal my nigga,"

Yolanda Simpson

"Smoke and pop this pill my nigga,"
"Smash a ho and make your dough—
that's how you keep it real my nigga."
But the real—
is that we're filling up jails.
Cops are shooting us like we're dogs,
and *we* do it as well.

Don't let the darkness try to tell you, it's light.
Don't let the wrong tell you, it's right.
Don't call it day when it's night.
And that money, that sex, that liquor,
it's a trap, so don't bite.
And the devil, he wants your soul;
get to seeing it right.

But God's plan—
it's for our boys to be men,
to share His kingdom with them,
deliver them from their sins,
to fix whatever's broken,
to give them legacy,
to make them fathers with honor
like they're supposed to be.
And when we act like they're less—
Yo, it be killing me.
I see them reach for the sky;
they hit the ceiling, B.
Between us and the cops,

it's like a killing spree.
I watch them die on the news,
like, "Is you kidding me?"
I wanna scream, "Don't let them...

Sex you up,
and get you high,
give you a gun,
and watch you die,
fill you with liquor, pills, stacks,
and watch you fly,
then steal your soul,
and watch you die.

Cause that's *the Plan.*
That's the plan for you.
That's his plan—the devil's plan,
the world's plan,
the system's plan for you.

Don't let 'em.

"For I know the plans that I have for you
says the Lord. Plans to prosper you
and not to harm you,
to give you a hope and a future."
(Jeremiah 29:11)

Initially published by Signet Music LLC
under the copyrights of Yolanda Simpson
as a part of the "Conflict" album (2019).

Yolanda Simpson

Sell Out

I'm gon' say this because I feel now
I'm talking about the money and the power and how
They gotta whole generation selling out.

You sold out for a gold tooth and a tat,
And a drug habit on your back;
And our babies they are watching and they're doing that
And they die and they kill and there's you in that.

Talkin' bout you're not a role model.
Yes you are,
And their bloods on your hand as you drive your car;
A generation of blood on your every bar,
You're like your father, the Devil, the fallen star.
You know, he's fallen?

Silly man,
Your profits are grand.
It's never gon' buy your soul back in the end.
Silly man,
What does it profit a man
To gain the whole world and lose his soul in the end?

Sell out, sell out, sell out!
You sell out!
For a quarter and a buck
You sold out,
You ain't talking about nothin'
You sold out!
Selling out your people, sell out!
You sold out!

SOOOOLD—
To the highest bidder!
Making Black people look like dumb niggas,
You make us look bad, while your pockets get bigger;
Teaching little girls how to be gold diggers.

About the money, it's all about the money;
It's all about the M.O.N.E.Y—and it's funny that,
After all the dirt you did,
You give your money to a charity called, "Save-A-Kid."
You could've saved them if you talked about something else;
You could have saved them
If you taught them to respect themselves.
You could of saved them, but you only care about your wealth.
You're getting paper, you're bragging. You shame yourself.

And you shame us,
And you shame the generations before us.
You shame the struggle and the prayers that delivered us.
Deliver us, deliver us...
Money's not a god.
Lord, please deliver us.

Sell out! Sell out! Sell out!

Big business got you shuffling *(Dance, boy)*
Record labels got you shuffling *(Dance, boy)*
Hollywood got you shuffling *(Nigger)*
They say, "Look at those Negroes shuffling" *(Spook)*
Look at those Negroes shuffling *(Dance)*
Look at those Negroes shuffling *(Boy)*
Why are Negroes shuffling?

IMAGE
Distorted and Discovered
Section 2

Bodies

Libby Young

What happens when the miracle inside of me,
    the one that gives life,
mars my existence with the edge of its knife?
Taking, not giving,
save only strife?

This vessel, this body, this fucking womb, a
field where only red flowers bloom
and bloom and bloom 'til they cover my grave, and
doctors will say it was a life that was saved.

"For you're so young and healthy;
you might change your mind.
You might wake up one day and find
that you want what you don't want,
and make another choice."

And I'll scream and shout 'til I have no voice,
yet it won't make a difference.
For I'm nothing.
I'm empty;
a vessel to carry someone else's hopes and dreams, who,
if a girl, will grow up to have silenced screams just like
mine.

Yet, she won't exist;
she won't be missed
by someone who doesn't even want her,
but only wants her own body back—
one that doesn't attack
her from inside.

Take it on;
suck it up.
It's not *that* bad,
Will the pain or society drive me mad?

For we are underfunded, understudied, under-researched, for
all my answers lie at the head of some church
who tells me that my curse is beautiful,
and to want something different
is just plain juvenile.

So, no matter the pain,
no matter the reasons,
I'll have to endure this
for all my life's seasons,
as what I want, can't be justified.

I'm just selfish, or lost, or broken.
I need to listen to men's tokens
of advice on how I should live
(which is to not);
and be thankful that I can give
life to a person not yet born,
while I die with all my dreams scorned.

I'm crying as I write this plea,
because I'm dying to be set free,
from this thing that has cost me decades of living,
from this thing that does nothing but shiv me
from the inside with pain and blood,
as it drags my ability to live through the mud.

This vessel, this body, this fucking womb,
this vessel has become my tomb.
So, place red flowers upon my casket;
take my question, and ask it—
Why can't I—why can't we—find any help?

Libby Young

Will there be someone to finally hear us?
Who can finally understand the fuss,
the noise and the hell
we've been raising?
Will there be light through the haze?
Will we live before we fade?

Can our bodies be ours first?
To choose whether or not we want to give birth?
Can the pain in our voices finally be heard
and not be made to appear fundamentally absurd?
Or disturbed?
Can we be taken at our word?

Two hundred and forty months have passed,
each one I hope is my last.
At thirty five, all I want is menopause
because,
this body of mine—
this miraculous creation—
can't even get herself an ablation,
much less answers to what is really wrong
or why has it gone undiagnosed for so damn long.

So, take heed, young things,
those about to mature,
there's only one thing of which you can be sure—
the choices you make only extend

to dinner plans and drinks on your weekends.
Your bodies are not your own,
not even when you become full-grown.

They belong to babies yet to exist,
or to men making demands with their fists,
or companies that don't even know you,
or lawmakers who just want to own you,
or thousands and thousands of online strangers who
will threaten you and put you in danger.
You'll be judged and demeaned and so much more;
you'll probably be called a whore,
but what you won't be able to do
is make a choice concerning you.

For those who still don't understand, I'll keep it simple,
I'll hold your hand—
this vessel,
this body,
this "beautiful" curse
has only ever made my life worse.

Libby Young

The Rage
Amy-Lenna Bryce

Fat Slut

Sometimes, I want to cut off
my breasts,
carve fleshy lumps
from my chest;

a slab of meat butchering itself.

They see the growth
of my cleavage as the
growth of my greed.
These organs

marbled with disgust,

offensive in existence, big
and frumpy;
displayed on a meat hook,
naked,
dangling like a ragdoll.
Or hiding
under shrouds of black fabric.

Even demure in dresses. They say,

"fat slut."

Skinned and raw,
I turn in on myself. Slicing
away the last sinews,

the cartilage of confidence,

preparing myself
for the judgmental meat market.

Undiagnosed

I don't remember when they diagnosed me, I was too young.
At 33, they have undiagnosed me.
I should be effervescent,
burdens dissolving like pills in a glass of water.
Instead I curl into my bed, sobbing
until it feels like my rib cage has unlocked and I am no more
than a vitrine of fractured dreams.
My ligatures have been cut, and now I'm drowning
in a hemorrhage of *what-ifs*.
My past divides,
a mitosis of memory;
imperfect copies of scenarios mutating
into a cancer of bitterness and rage.
A fictional history grows like a tumour until

I am once again 17 and typing my application for university.
I select all the places I have a secret burning desire to apply to;
the distance be damned.
At 18, I go to some far flung corner of the country and
stay up all night in libraries, find friends, join a sports team.
At 23, I visit Machu Picchu. Go to Nepal. Scuba dive around a coral
reef.
At 28, I allow my belly to swell,
not wondering if I will doom my child to a life

of watching her mother cough herself to death.

Amy-Lenna Bryce

I do not worry that my baby will have my illness.

When I cradle her in my arms, she is pink and furious in her
breaths,
not in a plastic pot, melting
into smoke and ash with the amputations, mastectomies,
and all the other clinical waste,

like she was in reality.
I want to reach inside my rib cage,
grab my lungs by their pristine airways and pull them out,
squeeze them like sponges,
try to wring out the life they denied me,
fling them at the feet of my doctors
and sprint away.

I have new dreams to chase.

The Rage

The rage lives
between my bones,
collecting in the dead
space,
in the gaps of my teeth
that I clench and grind until it hurts,
right up into my nose.

It is a jagged pipe dripping
into the dark of my brain,
pools of turbid water rattling with each drop.
The crust of rust,
flaking like old scabs on knees,
skinned and scarred
by the ghosts of trees
and bike rides.

It was injected into synovium
by stethoscope men
who scratch their beards and
shake their heads;
my mother bathed me in it,

and my father taught me to swim in it.

Amy-Lenna Bryce

Captain Kangaroo

Akin Jeje

Black, I tell ya,
I'm many years old,
Enough to recall
When breaking had soul.
B-boys an' b-girls on flattened
Cardboard boxes, helicopters,
Popses and lockses, Adidas,
Rope chains, rhymin'
Real Roxes, 50-odd years,
After the first robotics,
Hip-hop's third pillar is now Olympic.

Akin Jeje

Check it out, though, what these busters do,
You think they'd call up
Crazy Legs or Shabba Doo,
Naw, lookee here, it's Captain Kangaroo!

Step aside Large Professor, Professor X, KRS-One,
Today's Public Enemy's Professor Raygun,
In the house, heads is stunned, dunno if she's researchin',
Or just makin' fun, doin' that wallaby hop, she don't stop,
Doin' that wannabe...stop, please just stop.

Raygun, colonization, that ain't breakin',
It's appropriation, she got the shakes,
Like she's caught in a groove,
Iggy Azalea busts much better moves,
G'day, gimme Iggy any day,
Raygun's killin' us, but Iggy can slay.

Oh no hey-ho cheerio, watch Kangaroo Kathy goin',
Delirio, hail, hail the wannabe shero,
Judges so shocked,
They gave her straight zero.

Go kick rocks, you can't kick flavour,
Don't need another self-appointed white saviour.

Theorise, memorise, sermonise, moralise,
There's something deep Dr. Raygun don't realize,
You can't learn everything from a book,
Real breakers get down, they ain't weird,
They ain't shook. Breaking is an art,
A devotion, a culture,
Put THAT in your footnotes, you goddamn vulture.

Next time you misrepresent,
When real Olympians can't even pay rent,
Break south, shoo, Captain Kangaroo,
Flopping like a fish with its ass all bent,
Flailin' on the floor like your ass got sent,
Get off the stage- your notoriety's spent.

Akin Jeje

Damn the Light-Skinned Lottery
Carmen dela Cruz

Did I win? Did I win—the "light-skinned lottery?"
Am I a princess? Is it fair in the skin I am in?
Did I win, as the White man at the checkout stares at me,
my intricate box braids falling down my back,
boxed to break into African beats?
Then I hear the screech on the track
as he asks, "you usin' SNAP benefits?"
And I stare back blankly,
trying to remember what the hell SNAP is.

Did I win—privileged from a legacy of fair-skinned?
My momma and grandma now buried with secrets;
a grandma fair enough to pass, from the sins of a White man,
against her father's mother, but her father, a farmer,
thrived with a hundred Georgia acres,
sending Grandma and some of the other nine to college,
and I stand in this privilege, a legacy of Black educators.

Carmen dela Cruz

My father's people too: doctors, chemists, a mulatto sheriff,
chased through and out of Louisiana—
by cowards in white hoods—
to escape and build a generation of Arkansans.
But I am not in—not Black enough—
and too strong, too loud, to be White.
Did I win the Maureen Pearl lottery?
Brown eyes instead of *The Bluest Eye* or green, am I seen?
Or am I still in the shadows of crows that croak to a tune of Jim?

I should be soaring, not with cut wings,
silenced in shadows, my own voice clipped,
hiding behind the fear of a Black tax,
boxed in by unseen barriers.
Bullies once called me, "light bright" and "almost white,"
I hear you are not enough, not enough to lead,
when I came from Amazons, warriors, and scientists combined.

I am not a box to check, to be judged in degrees of blackness,
to spell out all the 58%, 38%, and the otherness ancestry
when my culture is 100%.
I make my own damn lottery.
And yes, I am a Black woman, light-skinned.

THE HEART
Love and War

Section 3

It Comes with the Territory
Courtney Seymour

"I couldn't see the harm until tonight."
Her hands ran red as
the words dribbled out;
a police officer holding the receiver to her ear.
"I know this seems crazy.
I didn't think he would cut in.
I thought he would get out of town.
I probably sound like
everyone you talk to."

I cradled my own phone at
the other end of the hotline, feeling
its hard plastic weight in my palm, feeling
the pulpy distance closing, wanting
to sponge up the mess and remorse.
She sounded like me.

"That doesn't seem crazy at all," I assured her,
twisting fingers through loops of phone cord,
jumping up and down for private emphasis.
"When your heart has glazed windows, it's an
impossible thing."

I want to say that I was ten when
I visited the Bronx Zoo and
got turned around in the prairie dog exhibit.
I might be wrong about this:
I sometimes confuse this trip with
a recurring nightmare of being stuck
like Alice, in a Wonderland hole too small
to allow me to grow.
I squeeze through passageways until
my so-big body can't move forward,
and I can't make the return
back to where it started.
I curl into the beaten ground,
eyes shut, wanting
to get out, wanting
to wake up.

A group of black-tailed prairie dogs is called a coterie.

A marriage to an abusive husband is called a codependency.
Both are exclusive companies,
but you have to know how not to be seen.

At the zoo the prairie dog enclosure
was built for trespass:
children from all the boroughs
would burrow, climb, up and out
of lucite tunnels
underneath the exhibit,
knees and elbows set at cut-glass angles,
clambering to touch daylight
in the observation domes dotting the lawn.

I cower in the darkness.
I can't find the right way for anything, and
left is right, bodies pressing,
with feet and fists to follow
me, stomped into a worn parenthesis of
yielding girlhood.
Eyelids squinched,
I say a little prayer:

Plexiglass figures
who are personable, kind—
watched from within and
without, innocents
trusting sanctuary,
trusting companionship.
Prairie dogs are vulnerable.
I am made of plexiglass.

Prairie dogs are a preyed-upon "keystone species."
Battered women are fair game for PTSD.
Locked into advers-or-pervers-ity,
it's essential that they both learn to bleed.

The White Queen would have remembered
which size I was once becoming and which thoughts
I would one day be growing, but I didn't know how to
make myself smaller or smarter,
only harder, like a chess piece
captured, like a child
in a plexiglass watchtower, where I see myself
chin to chest with the slightest and

softest-bellied of prairie dogs.
She calls out to me, a
muffled yip of solidarity.
Either she is checked or I am.
Either she is found or I am.

Once upon a time I was
a prairie dog, living
in a prairie dog town,
born into fiber-optic bloodlines,
calling through the night
and through the glass,

rooting for safety, for company,
wanting to be shatterproof,
wanting to be left, to be loved.

There's no name
for the crescent of earth that
rises to meet you when you matter.
There's no single path of refraction
when the shards have been scattered.

Female prairie dogs will guard their territories.
Survivors leave, but dare not speak their stories.
The male will bounce between his coteries,
broach women's trust and windows and believe
he sits atop the coiled edge
of food chains.

It's no wonder I was born afraid to dream.

Courtney Seymour

Bi-Bedtime Stories
Patricia Knight Meyer

Take this blank page of my body, write your script on me,
but please don't read my bedtime story. It's safer that way.
Read the one you write upon me, and I yours,
never stopping to open the book, to read beneath the pages,
to rhyme the truths of our twisted tales in Wonderland.
A safe read—to put us both to sleep.
But there is always more story to tell.
Questions left unasked.
Information withheld.
Truths whispering under the storybook covers—
or an enchanted frog, croaking, "I'm not what you think!"
Oh, but should I peek inside your rich binding?
Would I throw your story against the wall?
Shrink from your witchy bed, lacking a fairy tale ending?
'Cause in this story, Cinderella is wearing the other shoe,
and her Prince just might prefer stallions to pumpkins.
Oh, but should Sir Charming look
under his beauty's many mattresses?
Would he find that sweet pea of purity?

Or would he discover Snow White in the closet,
strangling a frog, and Cindi waiting for her on her knees?
Go ahead, wave your magic wand.
My body will tremble in your tempting bed.
Swirl me about your gallant castle
or tuck me away in your secret spire.
I might know the Kingdom's secrets,
but I am no town crier.
This little rider also has a following,
as she very well should.
The Bad Wolf pants as she passes,
to taste her sticky red hood.
She nods at the Butcher, the Baker.
She takes a taste of her pie.
She smiles at the Candlestick Maker
and flicks his thick wick of a fly.
So, go ahead and open it,
the storybook under your bed.
Open it wide and let's read it together,
and leave nothing more to be said.
Rub-a-dub-dub, Three Men in a Tub,
with bath bubbles high in the air.
Little Miss Muffet—he knew how to touch it,
and for him no one else could compare.
I will take the *Once Upon*, and you
can take the *Time*,
And we'll toss merrily beneath the covers,
with no reasons, just our rhyme.

Worms

Jon Jon Stefan

Maybe telling you I'm lonely is the reason you're distant.
You must have been trying your hardest.
Lonely was an insult at best.
My lonely was yours.
They hosted each other,
parasitized each other,
held each other,
and loved each other.

But we had nothing to do with them.
We lunch table-surveyed their little play dates.
Watched our cancers grow in our eyes
and envied them for loving us
and outliving us.

If just by some seconds.
If just by being the worms that run laces
from your cheeks to your lips to your teeth
without me.
Sowing your face to the soil
without me.

I wish I survived where they could survive.
I mean, I wish I could see
what they saw.
I wanna see what you look like
without lonely. I wanna see what you're like
under all of those vines.

You must have been trying your hardest for me.
Carving into a mirage in the desert.
I wonder if you found meat that bled when you bit.
I couldn't be mad if you knew me, then didn't.

Tsar Bomba

Criticizing poetry by being blind and lonely,
"all I am is love" reductionism;
all you are is over there—
so ugly.
All I am is held
between my thumb and my index
crushing my crush over there:

Tsar Bomba creates the sky for both of us

Tsar Bomba the blanket,
the umbrella above me,
the wince of romance behind me;
all I am just is
the part in Revelations where they called the police,
the last scene in forever,
where they jumped into a freeze frame.

All I am is Tsar Bomba

holding me like a pose;
I held her like a hallelujah,
like a mime holds a box.

Played

Yolanda Simpson

Tell me how you like it, baby,
   I'm not really trying to be here doing this, this way,
but he might stay with me;
ice me up and change my life.
If I play my cards right, maybe be his wife,
but I know better.

Baby. is it good to you?
It's not for me.
I can't believe that I feel so dirty.
Baby, is it good to you?
Don't wanna be another notch in your belt.

I played myself.

Yolanda Simpson

Should I respect myself?
Or should I lay with a man that I don't really know?
Maybe even infect myself,
with the H. with the I. or the V. or the D.
'Cause I want it to be love,
but I know that he don't,
but I know what I want
and I want it to be love,
'cause nobody ever really showed me love.
Show me love.

I don't feel like I'm nothing,
trying to feel like something.
I know that this fake loving, it ain't gon'
bring me nothing,
but pain and shame.
In another month. he will not know my name;
and I know, I know better.

Baby, is it good to you?
It's not for me. I can't believe that I feel so dirty.
Baby, is it good to you?
Don't wanna be another notch in your belt.
I played myself.

I know. I shouldn't do it, he's not the one.
I know, I know, I know,

I shouldn't do it, my life is going.
Out here playing games, I got played.
My life is gone, and my heart said not to do it;
should've listened to it.
Now I'm...

Ha Ha Ha–He's playing games.
I can play.
Yeah, watch me.
C'mon... Let's play!

Yeah, he's talking silky smooth.
He's about to make his move.
And I know what I'm gon' do.
I'm gonna give it to him, and–
I'm gon' juice him, and–
I'm gon' get him sprung, and–
I'm gon' be with him, yeah.

I'm gon' make him ice me;
I'm gon' make him wife me.
He's gon' take me to the mall.
He's gon' buy me nice things.
I'm gon' be his baby;
he gon' love me, maybe.
He gon' take good care of me.
I'm gon' be his lady.

Yolanda Simpson

What you mean, I'm pregnant and I'm
gonna have a baby?
What you mean, it ain't yours,
boy you must be crazy?
How you gonna leave me—
You know, boy, what you gave me?
Who gon' help me with this child?
How you gonna play me?

I know, I shouldn't do it.
He's not the one.
I know, I shouldn't do it.
Now my life is gone.
Out here playing games,
I got played.
I got played.
I got played.
I got played.
And my heart said not to do it—
Girl, don't you do it!
And now I'm wishing,
I wish I would've listened
But I played myself.

*Initially published by Signet Music LLC
under the copyrights of Yolanda Simpson
as a part of "The Verge" album (2011).*

The Mourning Dove

Monique Franz

In midday cool
drinking midday wine,
I watch two birds
on the fence—
mourning doves
in love—
or in lust.

The male stretches her-ward;
her neck leans away.
She plays hard to get
and fools no one;
he knows full well
she'll give in.

Monique Franz

The chemistry is tangible
I feel it from my rattan,
how it pulses
and rages;
a dance lingering
as it had all morning.

　　　She moves;
　　he moves
　　　　she inches away
　　and he pursues
　　　　　　　　she goes further
　　　　　　and so does he.

The female turns him-ward,
and their beaks touch,
their necks grind,
until she turns away bashfully.
He pushes in, more confidently.

This goes on for some time.
They look almost sick,
nauseous for one another—
chemically bonded
and emotionally
imbalanced.

In a flash—
his wing flaps
and he mounts her.
Vehement fluttering,
frantic flittering,
fierce flucking
for 3 seconds—
1.2.3
and it's done.
He's done;
they're done.

Maybe it's the midday wine,
the midnight fight,
or the midlife pain,
but I remember us
on our fence
years ago.

Your neck stretched me-ward;
my neck stretched away,
resisting your attention—
that potent tension.
I fooled no one,
and you knew full well,
I'd give in.

Monique Franz

Our courtship,
like these two mourning birds,
a fierce fluck
done in
seconds,
and all was done.
We were done;
you were done.

And I'm still here
on this fence,
a mourning dove,
mourning us,
having done hard time
for what was once
fierce,
frantic,
and fleeting.

Con-nec-tion

Floating,
  yearning
 neurons
desperate for
  connection.
Floating,
  loveless
 souls,
 longing
for affection.

Their lost
and
 wandering
  eyes
 begging
  in obsession;
questing for
  connection.
Zombie drifters
  reach
 for
  affirmation,
laying with
 other drifters,
adding

73

Monique Franz

       complications,
a blood-drawn covenant of
      loyalty
          ends.

Lovers   leave
       and friends
         "unfriend."

A devastating dis—
             con-nec-tion;
how brutal the dis—
        con-nec-tion.

I'm now searching
      for a pill
    to swallow,
for a sensation
    like love
      to mend;
         a faux form of
      con
         nec
     tion
    that requires
    no discipline
of effort

or
humility;

at best,
           its high
is short-lived.
But
true love
never fails.
Love,
the soul's connection to
Him
of whom Love is,
the source of Immortality
Infinity
Indestructibility—
Agape love.
As we drifters
             d r i f t
and sh ift, often jump-
       ing from a
            cliff,
His love remains unwavering,
Unmistakable.
Unfake-able—
UNBREAKABLE.

MENTAL HEALTH
Surrender or Conquer

Section 4

Cogs and Wires
Jon Jon Stefan

I'm wired dangerously

neutrons like cobwebs
catching onto nonsense
and blowing on the windowsill.

I'm wired constantly
burning in an outlet
but all without an outlet
don't let me near a kindle.

Still, I'm functioning—
cogs and wires—
fire as fuel to be fuel to fire
and before I cook myself, I can't be took
by these niche desires.

Jon Jon Stefan

I'm functioning, but how long for?
My warranty doesn't stand anymore
and I don't think I can stand anymore
of this function-less functioning forevermore.

Two into One into None

Mark Havlik

I must get out. Get out now!
  Piston-pumping crate careers on
taking me somewhere.
Why? Who's driving?
I can't see his face.
He won't turn, talk to me.
We are going fast—
much too fast, I think.

Out the window, I look.
A palette of brown.
Vines clustered, implacable,
strangle stout timbers.
Limbs vainly reach out—
the arms of the dying.
Rigor rushes in.
Mottled grass sleeps beneath
on hallowed ground.
Where is God's green?

Odd. No one is out mile after mile.
Not a solitary soul.
Where are the children? School is done.
They should be tossing a ball, dashing about.

Wait. Is that a church? It is.
I could speak to a priest. "Stop!"
     "For what? To say what? *Bless*
     me, Father, for I will sin."
He mocks me and keeps on.
I must get out now!

A shroud of gray looms ahead.
The sun beats on.
I blink. It's gone.
Have powered on. Ripped through
into shadow.
Barren, but for a blur of houses rooted in earth—
tombstones among the graveyards of wood.

Smoke?
The puff of white from a blooming cloud. No.
A wisp of fog, perhaps. No, no.
It *is* smoke, sailing high from a chimney.
A fireplace. Yes! So there *are* people.
Watching the flames streaming, retreating,
soaking in waves of heat. The embers pulsating.

That was how I left her the last time.
After balling on the floor, fused.
Her farewell.
Wanting it to be perfect.
As once, we imagined it could be.
Forever, I believed it would be.

We are speeding
like the years since I was with her.
                                    "Four."
But how can he know?
The months and days, he adds to it,
counting from the moment she ended it.
Not possible! I stopped, clocking it long before.
Senseless, really.

What am I doing here? Why did I get in?
Did someone force me into this hulk that drives on?
                                    "Someone did. But who?"
I am emptied of memories.
Only her, I keep in remembrance.
Nothing before, nothing since.
What has passed my past is beyond me.
Taken to the abysmal depths
by a marauding tide of melancholia.
Tomorrow, I have no use for—a weightless word.
It is all the same. Maddening monotony.
There is only now. I exist. That is what I do.
Here? Oh, no. An illusion is what I am.
Whatever is of substance—of me—
remains with her.

It grows darker.
I see only dots of light—dimmed, veiled.
Street lamps?
The road narrows. Becomes gnarled.
Jostling me about with every curve.
I must get out!
                              "That's not what you want."
"Why do you say that? I never told you."
                              "Oh, but you did."
Did I? Maybe this *is* my doing?
Why?
                              "You've wanted to take this
                                    ride."
When I hear that, I sense the faintly familiar,
but say nothing.
                              "Remember her touch on that
                              stormy spring night?"
"Oh, Christ, don't take me back there! Please..."
                              "Remember...?"
And how it sounds—a piercing scream,
though it is but a whisper.
I tremble.

The full of her hand pressed against my back,
through my shirt, my skin as if I were a body of water.
Her cradling my heart. Nothing said was as precious.
That spot is still tender where she slipped into me.

I must get out. I really—
                              "Calm yourself. Think of her...
                              always her... only her."

84

"I do."
Though she is all I remember:
there are sacred seconds of a yesterday
I fear casting my eyes upon.
Her hand on my heart is now a hatchet,
hacking, whacking, cracking through it.
                    "Ah... your eyes.
                    What *did* she tell you?"
Can he read my thoughts, too, this driver?
Who *is* he?
Surely, no angel. Devil, more likely.
                    "Those eyes..."
"Yes, yes, all right."
No need saying it aloud. He hears without my speaking.
A mirrored image is what I beheld of them.
Weathered as fallen acorns; and hers, two diamonds blue.
I asked—after she cooled from a scalding kiss—
uncoiled from my embrace—what it was about them?

"They see *too much* of me," she moaned, then rolled away.

Ever since I shut the door,
leaving her beside the fireplace, spent,
bundled in a blanket, rising to her breasts,
I have not dared to look at them. Not once, and never will.

We're on rougher road.
The bends sharpen. I brace myself.
This is not safe.
I hear him in my head.
Now it is he who does not need his tongue.

"How many times did they
demand your answer?"
He was there when I put myself
at the mercy of the mind probers—
plodding, poking, plucking the scabs away.
Pleased when they got to it—the raw patch.
"Too often, and you were.
But not always. Yes? Like now!"
"Yes, oh yes."
At last, he understands me.
I'm not safe. He'll stop. I must get out.
"And go where?"
He asks in a way I've heard before.
Precisely pitch-perfect.
"Back to your master
and you, the slave,
to his unanswerable question.
To *that?*"

I am beginning to recall why I got in...
where I told him to drive me.
Yes, I am sure of it.
"Take the wheel!"
I grab it. Two-fisted.
I can't get out.   I don't want to get out.

My foot rests heavy on the pedal. The road unfurls.
I'm climbing, and suddenly, a clearing.
Out of the clouds, into the mid-of-night.
Caressed alone by airy warmth.
Soaring! Sky riding!
Then silence.
Perfect silence.

The beacons blazing amid the brooding blackness,
floating free as the winged souls in Heaven beckon.
And I follow.

Mark Havlik

Wholeness

Carmen dela Cruz

W-h-o-l-e
and h-o-l-e.
Do we navigate a whole life
to find the different meanings of these words?
Navigating through what could have broken us;
a hole punched through a bathroom door
with my mother hiding behind it,
a hole wide enough for a small child to see,
a hole allowing the sounds of screams to echo off walls,
holes that will be hidden, patched, and carried for years,
not whole, not knowing what love looks like.
A hole that shows up in years of men who mirror casual cruelty,
cruelty that does not need fists,
but the wounds slice deep,
holes that need more than quiet reflection,
or speaking to a pastor or a priest,
holes that need the prayer, the guidance of a counselor,

so, when the hole that stops time comes,

and swallows you into a wormhole,

a reality of an alternate dimension,

you can't find your way back,

because can't you rewind the whole moment,

your junior year in college, the call from the hospital,

your mother, a heart so full of love,

a hole, an aortic tear,

not whole—"We did all we could."

Forty-six, a whole life not journeyed, a passport unstamped;

a hole as you look for her in the crowd at your wedding,

a hole as you give birth, looking for her hand,

her calming voice through the exhaustion and fear.

A hole as the doctor sews up your middle,

but the wholeness comes as your husband cuts the cord—

and your son cries,

wholeness from a heart

expanding,

expanding,

expanding as the nurse puts him in your arms for the first time.

Do You Have a Plan
Angela Gyurko

Could you seek
freedom in the tall trees
hardscrabble hills
meant to be climbed
by slender hooves
and fox feet
where wild food grows
for those who know
what to take and leave
no trace
for others to follow?

Or is the sea your safety
illusive as it may be
the fleeting dream of a boat
to other than this place
where war is a game children play
splashing on the beach
scaring away
the fish you must eat
with huddled masses
wondering who will start the
stone soup
and on whom you will cling
as your boat gets swamped?

Angela Gyurko

Will you hide
your safety found
with curtains drawn
windows dark
cans concealed
flour oil beans
the simplest of meals
hidden in your walls
hoping the bullets or shells
or whatever form this hell comes
will pass you
like in all the fairy tales
where one house
one family
survives the storm?

When war comes to you
which way will you flee?
Or more importantly
what did you do in
the days weeks months
before the first shot fired?

Final Destination
Tonnie MAC

Soon this train will come to a stop unexpectedly in the happy hour,
And the station is a thousand miles more, and yet not there.
The urge to go back and book again, but how?
True—nobody can know. Nobody will know
That Lions and bears cry too,
And they crave just
A little love and
A hug.

End?
Not yet.
Not yet the end,
Only the beginning to a
Long journey that I embark on.
I am sitting, looking, waiting for a train,
One that will take me to the far end—Dreamland.
One filled with the ethereal culmination of beauty unseen,
And in my holy mountain, none bruises another's feet on account of

The cruel weight that crushed the temple in the ruins of former Egypt.

None shall point a finger to the least of the unimportant, oh no.

None shall falsely accuse, even the condemned of *Misri*;

It is a world filled with wonder and beauty beyond,

And there we will cheer for a past forgotten,

Beauty that will make the soul merry,

Merry for a beginning of the end,

And end to the beginning of

The end of a long cry,

A flawless smile,

Beauty of the

End.

Last Supper

Why should I join your table?
Why should I intoxicate myself with,
the costly wine you flaunt with false splendor?
But in it, you slip a dose of lethal laughing toxins;
One would laugh and laud your generous tenacity.
Yet, with that fake giggle,
in the sunken, gleaming eyes of a snake,
you seethe inside.

We were a number, but the undertaker claimed a few.
Am I the only black sheep that feels the froth?
Or is everyone's heart blackened with drops of seeping venom,
that corrodes the lips? And you wipe the evidence.
Now that you noticed my awareness,
you turn the table for bile to flow from my quarter.
A good Samaritan, you'll offer gallons to quench the raging fire
and offer empathy to cure my ire.

You can burn my stiff,
but you won't my soul.
I will count the grains of sand in all beaches of the Pacific,
but to your corrupt course,
I shall never crawl.
Keep your mercy.
Every day, this team loses a player,
and you blame their folly.
Holy saints you are, but the acridity of bile will burn you all
when the reckoning of hypocrisy is finally done.

Child, Weep No More

I fought a dreadful monster today,
a grisly, horrific, and grotesque beast.
He mauled my heart as wolves would prey,
claws longer than swords minced the soul.
She froze my heart like winter east.
"*He's hungry for blood!*" Weep! Weep! Weep!

Only yesterday it ripped my hope apart.
In its grip of steel, he broke my bones,
crushed my head like a snake to dust,
not 'cause I didn't take enough calcium.
In fact, I baked in the sun all day.

Am sure that was enough. But *basking?*
No! I was sweating.
Plotting plans to pulverize the predators,
to break teeth sharper than surgeon's blades,
but broken bones and crushed souls?
Oh no! No! No!—Weep! Weep! Weep!

I fought a monster, but lost yesternight.
Its face scary and dreary;
it ripped my spirit to pieces
with no peace of mind to piece my pieces together.
I watched with tattered parts of my soiled clothes,
the ones that clothed my being.

It roared terror into my future.

I watched it rip my dad's relics, then throw them to the gutters.

I wept an ocean,

tears that washed my feet clean for a moment,

but I could not find the soap to remove the grease

of grief from my hands.

How would I bend to clean my feet with greasy hands?

In no time I ran scared for my life

in the mud again.

Oh no! No! No!—Weep! Weep! Weep!

Now, I have no one to help.

I sit by the deeper mud,

and shed more tears,

from these empty tear glands again.

Gosh, I miss him—

I never had the chance to bide a wee.

How would he be now?

How many lives would he have saved by now?

The awaited master's in medical biology class,

but never got to graduate.

Wasn't I too young to fight the monster?

But I didn't need strength of hands to win.

I had the strength of mind,

Tonnie MAC

I had the unwavering spirit.
I had the good of heart.
I had the determination.
I... I... I had nothing, but still went on.

And I took a hoe; I went to the mines.
Yes—into the deepest and darkest mines
with a goal to dig,
to dig the gold of good, but not the past.
And of determination,
and of unwavering fortitude.

Today, I am fighting a monster.
Today, I must win.
He has ripped a heart,
splinted a spirit, and crushed a soul.
The monster has chewed my legs;
I can run no more.
In fact, I crawl on the ground,
in the mud of desperation—
back and forth, back and forth—
the mushing mud maddens my mind.

But I have to crawl;

I have to row to the light.

Why does he drag everyone

to his side like death?

Is there no warrior?

I must defeat.

Kill the monster.

Either way,

I have to win

this war for us all!

Scared and scarred,

I come in courage.

Weep! Weep! Weep! Weep no more!

Tonnie MAC

The Truth

Lucy Collins

D efine "okay."
Make it into a word that isn't just said to save face,
a lullaby to soothe the minds of those who couldn't care less.
When all they need to do is press,
they don't.

I say it to skirt around the solemn subject,
I say it to take your mind someplace else.
Don't let it haunt you,
−when I'm gone−
you'll know I meant something entirely different.

Lucy Collins

Spoken like a true con artist,
this is what a breakdown does to you:
weaving between words,
interlacing them with false hope
because I so want it to be true.

I say nervous,
instead of psychotic.
Build up walls
on a foundation of lies,
hating that I was sick.

Strength doesn't have to come in numbers,
it often encumbers,
letting you in can be a solo venture
when it banks on that one word.
Well, I'm up for the adventure:
it's for the resilient,
or so I've heard.

I've come so far,
and yet it still haunts me.
The past is still clear to see,
but if that's what you want to hear–
then fine.

I'm okay,
and sometimes–I actually am.
This wasn't meant to be a ruthless slam.
I'm stronger than I was,
but that came at a cost.

You say I'm robust
just because of the colour of my skin;
I break just as easily.
I was the size of a pin.

Pain can be insufferable,
making you wish for a life that's more tolerable.
I'm relieved that I won't be sent away,
and today, I feel my own version of "okay."
But don't ask me to define it,
or else, as you can see,
I'll go off on one.

HOME

Heritage and Pride

Section 5

Home

Carmen dela Cruz

Home is a gravel road,
    paved with chunky grey rocks,
a dust that rises like smoke,
settling thick on cars,
lingering like the voices of the past,
a house sitting on a couple of acres,
where neighbors were not close,
and the screams inside could not be heard,
the laughter of the children, mired by those screams.
the dogs came running,
running to her in the yard,
the garden sang at her touch,
my mother, mother to all things—kind—
but unable to escape the darkness on the road,
the dust, the cloud gathering as the car pulled up,
and those hands larger, stronger than she.
Through the fog I can't see it,
the rocks washed in tears,

Carmen dela Cruz

painted in hues of grey, blue, and purple.
Home, but I can't—
can't go back there.
Too afraid that I might choke on what lingers,
shut behind doors of the abandoned house,
abandoned memories.

but my home
is also the warmth of a grandma's hug,
summers with the sweet smell,
the crackle of catfish frying in her special breading,
a red brick house, sturdy and strong like she,
to protect children from all the storms,
the screams miles and miles away,
wrapping us in the warmth of quilts long made with love,
wrapping us tight and snug,
so we can breathe, so we can dream.

This Soil in My Blood
Lola–La Revolution–Rosario

The land of my birth is not my homeland
nor is it yours, though history books say otherwise

they speak of an Abraham and a George
tall tales of e-man-ci-pa-tion and a tree

from whose sturdy branches your ancestors
mercilessly took the last breath of mine

leaving me with nothing but twigs of trauma
another unrooted soul searching for heritage

something to call my own–a lineage unborrowed
not yet colonized–a tongue still proudly native

defying mighty swords intent on erasing all identity
substituting their culture with your vicious crown

Lola—La Revolution—Rosario

to pillage and massacre, calling it discovery
fabricated by domination, you took what was theirs

until their riverbeds lay barren of any remnants of gold
those once clear waters turned crimson-colored

and of those who survived, to meet a different fate
now clothed and bearing a cross, you claimed them free

to live as they chose, but stripped of their very essence
your diseases and greed stifling their existence

they remained shackled to a so-called extinction
becoming a mere footnote in the annals of your conquests

a valiant and noble people, forever a colonial cleansing
repeat all your untruths until none of it is questioned

each passing generation becoming more willfully ignorant
blinded by the oppressors' pervasive shadows

in hopes we would never find a path toward our light
the kind that has always illuminated who we are

and though today your descendants insist on denying
the valor of my forebears, hoping to stain their memory

I continue to resist your watered-down version of Ourstory
because the whispers of my ancestral motherland echo

This soil in my blood.

When You Ask Me Where I'm From

When you ask me where I'm from,
I will point to a place on the map:
a tiny archipelago in the Caribbean,
the richest of ports we still call Borikén.

I will tell you I come from a valiant + noble people
who worshiped the sun + the moon;
hunter-gatherers who knew not waste
whose kindness was mistaken for weakness.

When you ask me where I'm from,
I will call out the names of our warriors
the brothers Agüeybaná I, Agüeybaná II (El Bravo)
as well as the only female Chief on our soil,
La Cacica Yuisa.

I will speak to you of a land once abundant
in cacao, cane sugar, tobacco + tropical fruit
where they harvested their own food
and had zero need for anything exported

Lola—La Revolution—Rosario

When you ask me where I'm from,
I will share with you stories of our African
ancestors who gave us intoxicating
drum beats + added to our flavorful cuisine
reminding us what it means to carry
their rich heritage in our veins.

I will show you images of our
pristine shores + verdant countrysides.
I will speak to you of the warmth
of my prideful People.

When you ask me where I'm from,
I will say all of these things because
though a foreign land birthed me
my heart has always belonged to
Borikén.

They Call My People Resilient

because we have survived five centuries of colonization
through genocide of our Indigenous Taíno and Iñeri
lived through thefts of our lands
and sterilizations of our women
fought a foreign invader bringing a false banner of freedom
protested against the Foraker Act
 and the Jones Act and the Gag Law
and Ley 22, now Ley 60, and Obama's PROMESAS
and La Junta's Fiscal Control Board cutting teacher's pensions
and closing over 200 public schools

They Call My People Resilient

for not losing our minds over the massacres at Ponce
and Río Piedras and Utuado
Cayey and Sabana Seca and Cidra
and Carolina and Mayagüez
because we continue
the relentless struggles against displacement
land grabs and destruction of our natural resources to build
apartment complexes for foreigners to continue colonizing
and gentrifying our sacred soils

They Call My People Resilient

Lola—La Revolution—Rosario

because of Hurricanes Georges and Hugo
and Irene and Irma and María
because they learned how to make due
with nothing but blue tarps
to barely cover leaking roofs
and struggled for weeks and months with limited access
to clean drinking water and
figured out how to survive with no electricity
for 100 days while a corrupt government
 made a mockery of the suffering
of the poor and minimized the death count

They Call My People Resilient

as if it were a badge of honor, something to be proud of
          –a prized trophy
to show off how strong and capable
we are of dealing with endless injustice
and discrimination, attacks and abuses–
when what we're really doing is honoring the legacies
of our warrior ancestors who fought without complaining
to overcome impossible odds to simply
survive

Code Switch

subconsciously processing surroundings & situations
molding our environments to fit us ~ we are spacious
round wholes
not needing pegs too square for the sounds of our
kinda wonderful
making music out of made-up words once considered too foreign
for ears unaccustomed to soooo much flavor & richness
taking them on a lexical ride of
roller-coaster the mind
expressions restructured no longer nice & tidy
        ~ ¿Tú sabes what I mean?
or maybe you don't understand this
more-than-monolingual mind
too active for your halls of knowledge ~ we are a vernacular
linguistically legitimate
a place where inglañol and spanglish are always celebrated
where interpreters & translators are unnecessary because
our language is our safe space, a place where the doors are
always open

She

shy child
middle child
bullied child
get good grades child
don't answer back child
fear her father child
not quite good enough child
unprotected child

She was the

"You and your drama" daughter
"You're just like your father" daughter
"You're never satisfied" daughter
"Why are you so difficult?" daughter
"How many times are you gonna
make trouble in this family?" daughter

She was the

doesn't remember you ever hugging her child
the why didn't you ever remind her how intelligent,
strong and beautiful she was? child
the your sons were all that ever mattered to you child
the there is zero memory in her heart of you ever
saying the words *I love you*

She was that kind of child

The one who grew up and turned into
an entirely different kind of person

She turned into

the confronting her childhood traumas woman
the no longer afraid and no longer broken woman
the, yeah, she went to therapy cause *ain't no shame
in asking for help*–that kinda woman

the one who knows she gotta love herself
first, second, third, and all the way down the line
the one who speaks her truth
because lies are too BUR-DEN-SOME kinda woman

She quickly became the

wears her heart on her sleeve
but do NOT get it twisted because
she ain't nobody's fool kinda woman
the not gonna smile in your face
when you say some stupid shit kinda woman

She is now

the only surrounding herself with beautiful
kind and compassionate beings

Lola—La Revolution—Rosario

the she is PERFECT in her imperfections
kinda woman

Today she stands before you as
the she knows her worth kinda woman
the every second evolving into the most
amazing She

the, yeah, she's all that and a bodega
full of chips kinda woman

How do I know all of this?

porque esa mujer, that woman,
right there–She
is ME

Uncle Sam's
Walt Shulits

I t was squalor one might expect in Karachi or Kabul but not
in a hinterland hamlet in Kansas, a once-bustling burg now
little more than a graveyard for industrial dinosaurs.

its air still blackened and barely breathable, the parking lot
of this particular property pitted, potholed and reeking of piss,
varicose veins of coal tar

bubbling up under the laser-like sunlight, all that oozing
goo sticking to the tired treads of second-hand Subarus,
suctioning to worn soles of Walmart sandals and sneakers,

then curdling and collecting on the crumbling concrete steps
leading into Uncle Sam's, its once sleek stainless steel silver
bullet shell now dulled and dented,

desecrated by defecating doves, any remaining dignity
obdurately dying like a fiftyish former femme fatale
fearfully facing her future.

Walt Shulits

Uncle Sam's had been more than just a diner; it was
a pantheon to patriotism where for decades Old Glory
was reverently raised and lowered each day,

where humility and civility accompanied hard-earned
social mobility, where veterans were heroes, free meals
offered and fund raisers organized for those

the VA left behind, where the community congregated to
celebrate the high school basketball team making the state
tourney, free chili dogs and sodas for all the kids,

a pitstop for pandering politicians peddling promises and
proposing policies they'd promptly forget upon parting
Uncle Sam's after pigging out on pecan pie,

a place where a college French professor and the town's
trash truck driver talked trout fishing over glazed donuts
and a cup of Joe, where Johnny ordered

a moon pie and Vanilla Coke after football practice and
didn't have to worry about someone stealing his Schwinn
Sting-Ray, where you could order waffles 24/7

and they'd arrive groaning under two mountainous gobs
of melting butter soon to be submerged by a torrent of
Vermont maple syrup—grease was good, a gift from God,

gimme some hash browns and sausages with them waffles—
a place where a single mom could treat her kids to a cheap
mac and cheese after her shift at the cannery and

new arrivals from Mississippi and Alabama, black and white,
were welcomed with open arms, the factories eager for
workers to keep the country's industrial juggernaut rolling,

the local folks united in the belief that there would always
be an American frontier, that everyone could earn a decent
wage, own a home and retire in relative comfort,

confident that their children's lives would be even better and
the nation would remain a beacon beckoning all those willing
to work and contribute

...but today Lady Liberty winced as she surveyed what
remained of Uncle Sam's, a montage bleaker than
a Hopper painting or a Steinbeck novel,

a panorama that lent itself less to a Bruce Springsteen
ballad than the plaintive pleas and confessions of a
sloshed Tom Waits rasping and writhing on the floor

or an expletive-laced rant by rapper Nicki Minaj who could
be excused for her vicious vitriol because she had never
known the good times and her people had been excluded.

Entering the diner was like trudging into a mausoleum or a nearly
empty casino, where the remaining players were tapped out, too
poor to even spin the wheel and simply sat there stunned,

trying to remember the last time they actually harbored hope,
the few cha-chings of the slot machines, just the occasional
clattering of cheap chipped plastic cups,

plates and utensils all manufactured in Asia—like everything
else these days—the flagless flagpole at the entrance listing,
buckled over like a blottoed bum about to barf,

the Formica counter a miniature bomb crater, yellowed, chipped
and pitted, pocked with cigarette burns, puppy love initials
carved 40 years ago no longer legible, the once luxurious

leather booths and counter stools succumbing to years
of being squashed by big-butted, beer-bellied bankers,
butchers—even beauticians—launching themselves

into their seats like elephants bouncing up and down on beach
balls, the subsequent decision to recover the furnishings in fake
maroon crushed velvet with gold trim practical, but

rousing the ire of the Catholic Diocese and the local chapter of
the Young Republicans Federation, both groups bewildered,
embittered that Uncle Sam's might become a bordello.

They shouldn't have worried: decades into the diner's decline, the
meme that most epitomized the hopes and promises of the past,
in stark contrast to the pathos and pessimism of the present,

was a vintage vinyl-playing Wurlitzer jukebox from Uncle Sam's
grand opening in 1948, regurgitating all those golden oldies
from a glorious but long-gone era:

"California Girls" by the Beachboys, Steppenwolf's "Born to
be Wild," and who else but the Beatles' "8 Days a Week," this
time capsule, now visited maybe three or four times a year

by sentimental septuagenarians and not yet carrion octogenarians
who chuckled as they hummed along to the Monkees' "I'm
a Believer," the rest of the barely sentient beings in Uncle Sam's

too angry or depressed to do anything but mine the internet for
fearsome, but frequently fallacious factoids, or to tweet tantalizing
untruths, venom to validate their vindictiveness, absolve them

of any responsibility for their possibly, perhaps even probably,
preventable plights, a brotherhood of the bedraggled and
beaten brazenly rebuffing blame... but permit me

to posit plausibly that a plurality of these poor people
were powerless pawns preyed upon by piggish plutocrats,
prejudiced police, prevaricating politicians pocketing payola

from licentious lobbyists; they were easy targets for hateful
harangues by heinous homophobes, right wing racists or those
pedantic progressives pretending to play Robin Hood,

both sides preaching partisan poppycock on polarizing pod-
casts to these remnants of a rampant runaway capitalism that
had exterminated mom and pop stores,

replaced assembly lines with hordes of humanoids, rapacious
robots that ran roughshod over the few remaining workers,
mainly retiree wannabes—no healthcare despite their pleas—

paid less than teenage trainees, forced to live in ramshackle
RV's—only cheap Chablis to numb their misery... while Silicon
Valley CEO's were not the least bit concerned

their own pay 300 times what their workers earned,
pensions, unions and a higher minimum wage spurned,
discussions on employee ownership abruptly adjourned...

but what a pity that San Francisco had gone from pretty
to gritty to pretty shitty to a tent city, the billionaire class
while babbling about biomass became combatively crass

demanded the riff-raff get off their ass, quit smoking grass,
stop complaining and get some job training—but given their
economic degradation: who could afford relocation?

Meanwhile capitalism's oligarchs indulged in a feeding frenzy
that would make Moby Dick proud; the jerks smirked at the
endless perks allegedly rewards for their "hard work"—actually

just access to leverage even as their companies hemorrhaged—
perks like flying in private jets while piously paying carbon offsets—
or buying island nations, the locals, victims of gentrification.

One tech titan demanded a European capital take down a bridge
so his mega-yacht could pass, while another tried to buy Mount
Rushmore to carve his own magnificent mug into the mountain

as several others risked their carefully cultivated auras
of omnipotence in a race to open the first hotel on Mars—if
shuttle fares were $250,000 imagine the room rates...

but the besieged brethren of Uncle Sam's couldn't worry
about San Francisco or the fight for Mars; they were victims
of a shakedown caught in a social meltdown slowly dying

in an industrial ghost town, suffering the opprobrium of fiscal
pandemonium—hell, they could command the podium at a
symposium on the odium of the schism from neoliberalism—

no Friday happy hours since their lives had soured, water too
toxic to even take a shower, and how about that ice storm that
left Texas without power. Absolutely anyone could buy a gun

but if you needed an abortion you were on the run from bounty
hunter religious zealots empowered through courts appellate;
even in the case of rape, there was no escape, but what

really grated was politicians never hesitated to cut corporate
tax rates, despite the need to dissipate the rupture in the nation's
infrastructure, to give reassurance

to the 10 percent with no medical insurance, to finally address
the distress of the homeless. Why was there always money for
wars on foreign shores when many so-called allies

were diplomatic whores and what about the stiff-lipped
silence when we supported tyrants, the ferocity of the
hypocrisy when we claimed to be defenders of democracy?

Uncle Sam's was nearly empty, the new normal in an economy
not yet near its nadir, only five sullen stone-faced customers,
staring into space, mostly suffering in silence,

each wanting as much distance as possible from the others as if
their affliction was contagious, that the country was suffering
from a systemic epidemic to which only the rich were immune.

Jada was dismayed now unpaid after the principal's tirade;
no longer could she teach, impeached for a material breach
of a school board rule—refusing to carry a gun in school

because nothing should imperil the right to bear arms
so schoolmarms had become gendarmes to limit the
number of kindergartners harmed.

She had $70,000 in college debt, eviction of this single mom
a constant threat, no longer having a medical plan threatened
her asthmatic daughter's lifespan, because if an attack

called for urgency, they could only go to emergency, which
meant all the fuss that came with riding the bus since
given her financial morass, she couldn't afford to buy gas.

Harold sat hunched, hunkered down in his Houston Astros
hoodie, hands hidden in the pouch pocket, sweat-stained,
backward baseball cap, guillotining his ears,

stuck in a situation risible, a man child desperate to be
invisible, knew he was no Jobs Zuckerberg Bezos Gates
or any of the other reptilian reprobates

but dreamed that the stock options he'd been granted—
his salary they'd supplanted, and now he was left de-panted,
oh, how he rued that day, he'd been led astray,

now he had to pay for his naïveté—would make him wealthy
at a tender age, so he upscaled his tastes and now was
ashamed, but there was no one else to blame,

feeling demeaned to be seen in Uncle Sam's having grown
used to Starbucks, GrubHub deliveries, slim-cut J. Crew suits
with reverse collar dress shirts and candy apple Pumas

until Visa, Mastercard, and American Express all blocked
his cards leaving him mired in credit muck, drinking drain
cleaner coffee that gave him reflux—oh how poverty sucked—

before heading home to his bed in his parents' garden
shed. He'd never own a home, would end up alone, so why
not invest his unemployment benefits in meme stocks?

Sophia was born in America to illegal immigrants, their
deportation always imminent, but content to work jobs
undocumented, something southern Republicans resented,

pathetic hours and pitiful wages willingly weathered—anything
to keep their family together—Sophia slaving as a machine
operator, all the mill's misogynists lusting to fornicate with her,

and several nights a week as a bartender relying on tips from
the big spenders, trying to earn enough for tuition to bring her
college dreams to fruition, but then came

the dreaded knock at the door—the family unit was to be no
more—and when the mill and the bar both shut down, there
was very little left of the once vibrant town,

leaving Sophia alone and jobless, with no further access to
government largesse, suddenly pregnant in a state, where
there was no debate—abortion was absolutely apostate.

Walt Shulits

The two bulbous bearded brothers in the booth seething and
sneering at Sophia had swastika neck tattoos and buck naked
babes on their forearms. Bill and Phil were twins,

former marines dishonorably discharged for drunken assaults
on "spics," "niggers," and "faggots," then fired from jobs at the
cannery and textile mill for the same hair trigger rage.

They were nativist, there'd be no cease or desist, they simply
couldn't resist adding transgenders to their list, chuckling about
beating the wee wee out of "he-shes" and anyone else

who dared disagree with the political philosophy of blaming those
billionaire bastards and the babbling bureaucrats, their lobbyists
bought for the lack of decent jobs for Caucasian citizens, and

there were too many violent, welfare-reliant immigrants, and how
in hell did the woke faction get the traction to pass affirmative
action—no, just call it "Blackion," a civil rights of Whites in-
fraction—

while they vandalized statues honoring true American heroes...
the nation needed a wall to forestall democracy's downfall
and maybe reservations like for the Navajo nation, you know

stick those people in the desert like tumbleweeds, give 'em casinos,
and let cheap booze and slot machines keep 'em out of trouble...
but the twins wanted a quicker solution, an Aryan ablution,

so Bill and Phil and thousands of their patriotic bros and sistahs
were planning a little shindig in Washington—assault weapons
obligatory—to convince Congress of the errors of its ways.

Five forlorn figures, five profiles in futility, fearful except for the
feckless brothers who were feverish for a fight... all feeling
slighted, their existences blighted, so nearsighted

they were oblivious to the possibly perfidious events going down
in their little corner of the obliterated town, home prices taking
a beating as borrowers besieged their bankers bleating,

but a Saudi Arabian sheik found the prices addictively cheap,
bought several properties each week, including the cannery
and mill—they were destined to become landfill—and finally,

the linchpin of his plan, he approached the third generation
owner of Uncle Sam's with an offer he couldn't possibly reject,
his finances completely wrecked, no chance to resurrect,

the sale a secret he kept as he wept and rarely slept, because
the sheik had shared an inkling of his strategic thinking: the town
was sinking, its population shrinking, he'd outlaw drinking

and make the municipality a Mecca for Muslim migrants with a
mosque where Uncle Sam's now sat, no more Wurlitzer record
player, just the doctrinaire call to prayer... burkas obligatory.

"Oh, beautiful for spacious skies for amber waves of grain..."

We A-OK, USA
Diego Alejandro Arias

Nada, Nunca, Always.

I tell you this—that no other can find us.
That we have no mouths
and no eyes
and no hands
and we are to swim across the Atlantic, and find the ghosts
of men and women and children and patriots and journalists and
the people scream @ you and me and us, and they say
"The communists and rabid, crazy, wild-eyed bandits will tear
everything apart.
And the economy will falter
the sky will turn a color red."

Diego Alejandro Arias

And it happens nunca;
a nadie le importa.
Pero death, ah yes, the death squads enter
the amazon and they shoot to kill.
The voice of the people, trapping the box
digging a hole
and saying, "We killed the terrorists. They will never return."

We A-OK, USA

Lots of brown people drowning in soup.

Many many White women heroes, champions of the cause

but won't let a migrant worker sit down next

to them on a bus, because he is still

still

still

a predator, a dirty hand,

mustachioed monster that mows her lawn

and his wife washes her clothes

and Bangladeshi children make her clothes

and Korean women press her clothes

and Ukrainian women liberate her clothes

and Black women ask her

"Will you support our cause?"

She says

"No. Not right now. Let's wait.

Do not agitate.

Do not make a scene, brother. Do not—do not

make a scene, please—I beg of you.

Work with what we've got."

But

But

But

never let you finish a goddamn sentence.

Diego Alejandro Arias

Even White Latina women
go on MSNBC and talk
the Empowerment
Pero we all know that sister girl has never
had no noxious gases in her power suit.
Even her power is half-revolutionary
half-keep-your-voice-down
half-young man, half-a-change-is-coming, let's just
wait and see what happens, just you
wait now, wait, wait, on these men
to make it right now
sitting at the table
very serious person doing very serious things.
She is now the
man that sat next to her
on a bus, and she says
"We are the change the world needed."
And the people rejoice
and they die. They die. They fucking die.

La Mas Bonita del Barrio

And I ain't talking about a girl;

We're talking 'bout a house, like the nicest on the block.

All the White people look at it and say, "Who lives there?"

And then, they see me

in my military shirt, hoodie, leather jacket,

looking like an extra in Belly.

Remember that scene with DMX and Nas?

Where they wearing all that cool ass shit?

And the neighbors ask,

"How did this man throw down the cash,

get over the interest rates,

get over the credit scores, and the seller's brick wall,

and his or her bullshit brainwashed mediocre

White man nonsense?"

But they don't see the 800+ 辣酱油 transunion points.

They don't see the 24 years of education,

the eight years of white house politickin',

The higher-er-er-er annual salary,

better than the average White man

In New Jersey; higher-er-er-er than the gentleman in

southern England,

down the Cotswolds, where men in horses roam around

wild rapeseed flowers.

Diego Alejandro Arias

And here I am, this war-born, grease-and-oil-hand,
chicharron eating papasito.
Gets to live the American dream
and own what my father wanted when he
crossed the border with sand from Mexico in his pants,
and bullet holes in his buddies' bodies,
because the DAS had bullseyes on
his union-loving, Banana Republic fighting ass.
But demons do nada;
devil never bothered to hold onto my legs.
I pulled, swam through so much muck and mud and dust
and violence, so much boomer economic philosophies.
I got the nicest house on the block,
la más bonita del barrio mi hermano.
Believe that.

OUR FOREFATHERS

Sins and Wins

Section 6

I Blame My Ancestors
Jonathan Chibuike Ukah

When the White man came to our home,
and seized our land with guns and bayonets,
with the moon moaning, the sun scorching
as the stars shed their lights at noon,
we were like them that drank the Red Sea
without crossing on dry ground when it split.

My ancestors stared at him with saliva gushing,
as if he arrived from the sun as the Sun God.
They touched him to feel his silky skin,
gleaming in the daylight like eggshells;
they stared into his eyes to see the bluebell
spiraling in his iris like a lavender garden,
like he was a king from birth.
They kissed him on the lips like he was a lover,
invited him to their houses like he was a god,
sent to them to answer to their ablution.

Jonathan Chibuike Ukah

They gave him food like he was famished
and they were gaping and sowing seeds.
They carried him on their lean shoulders,
like he was their baby going into his crib,
and swooned over him like he was their angel.
They worshiped him, like he was their saviour,
and fought for him like he was their master,
whom they must serve—or die imprisoned.
In the end, they gave him their land,
like he was their inheritor, their heir,
or a bishop destined to build a church for them.

My ancestors cuddled the White man
like a long-awaited torrential rain,
without cuddling their lonely gods.
They fed him without feeding their gods;
they did not joke with him,
but joked with their gods on their sofas.
They opened their hearts to embrace him like a gift.
Through their palm leaves, their oil,
they clothed the White man like birds of the air,
rendering their gods naked and freezing.
My ancestors forgot to pay them homage
and offer libations to the keeper of their lives.

They went to bed and woke up at dawn,
muttering the White man's words and lyrics,
filled with his songs, dancing to his music.
They abandoned their home, wine, and food—
the little things that made a god birth miracles,
go for long walks on the beaches of their rivers,
on the sun-soaked beds of their gardens.
They dropped ornaments of beauty and charm
on the pawpaw thighs of the White man
and fretted their ancient gods to deep groans.
My ancestors worshipped the White man's God.

When I was born, there was light
steeped in the deep waters of my mother,
but my father welcomed me like a stranger,
as though I travelled and returned,
as though I were a child best becoming the tide
through which my ancestors pushed the waves
down the throats of a raging life.
I didn't know why.
I realised I was face to face with my parents' teeth,
tucked in their closed mouths, but shining through,
glistening like pieces of Nzu from the Nri
of my ancestral home, where I was an umbilical.

Jonathan Chibuike Ukah

My mother's teeth sparkled on our roof,
like dazzling crystals on a seashore.
My body was a shore, the extension of the river,
through which my ancestors travelled
to find themselves in memory graves,
in the house where I was born.
My father's teeth rested between iron chains,
as if he planted cactus seeds on a White man's head;
as if his mouth broke into shards like volcano rocks,
as if in the absence of the White man,
death hung in his closet like underwear.

I didn't want to tell them this nightmare,
that I had swallowed the cry of their gods
night after night, in the depths of my throat.
Often, I felt their hearts bleeding like a sacrifice,
and their blood gushing through my fingertips.
Their laments sliced through my heart like a stroke
in a shrill echo of the groans of a python,
which witnessed the massacre of its children,
their blood sprayed along the path of its departure.

For the desolation, for the cry in the wilderness,
the lament of the bluebird, the weeping of the python;
for the flowers that withered in summer,
and the death in winter mornings and nights,
for the desertion of the sun on our shores,

for this darkness creeping into our houses,
through the cracks they have carved in time.
For the graves that littered our paths,
the chasm into which we found ourselves
among wet stones still dripping with blood,
where we breathed hard like a tree climber,
running away from a snarling snake
about to snatch the last vestiges of his soul.

For the lies told to our children, their faces suffused
with the distortion of truth and facts.
For the history we lost, the way we were abandoned
for deserting their gods and donating our inheritance
into the uncharitable arms of the White man;
for folding their arms across their heaving chest
as though it was not their war, this looming fracas,
this dark cloud engulfing our nation, our hearts,
this cankerworm seeping like a disease into cavities
which their neglect, greed, and selfishness had created.
For this looming massacre of the young;
this destruction happening, the dead ancestors laughing
at the ubiquity of their shadows, the horror,
that death has certain pride in sorrow.
For the tears of the dying, their silent sobs;
for the unheard sound of prayer of the helpless,
those slumped into the trenches of blood,
where only death kisses them goodbye,
I blame my ancestors.

Jonathan Chibuike Ukah

A Panegyric to My People

To those I lost in the First World War,
who went to arbitrate between masters,
who travelled from the deserts of the Sahara,
where raindrops teased their bodies
and were smuggled into pockets of snow,
to ward off the imminent coldness of their masters' feet;
to them, I drop this tear like a spear,
that pierces through the fabric of my soul.

To the murdered, the slaughtered,
the shamefully assassinated and the wounded;
those incarcerated on their march to freedom,
martyred for asking the right question,
for believing that all men were born equal,
and to be honoured in life and death,
and have the inalienable right to the same bullet.
There is the right to die by the same means,
the right to live to die; the right to die to live,
when departing is the favoured return
of the thousands who are porous to belief.
There was stubbornness in your obedience,
a stubbornness to witness the mortality of the master,
to prove your point, to assert that all men,
born through the pains of a woman, are equal,
and for whom no star and no comet appeared
to herald either a first or a second coming.
To you, my people, I raise this glass of heroism,
and implore you to drink it in remembrance of us.

To those I lost in the Second World War,
those who toiled and toiled through the night,
and through their labour, became kerosene,
formed an alloy with the oil of the lanterns,
went into the sea at night, searching for fish,
and caught nothing till daybreak;
those for whom the war was an escape, a ruse,
because no master told them to cast their nets
where the water was deep and the fish congregated.
No one to recruit them as fishers of men,
and the only salvation that fell on their soft thighs
became a war of mispronunciations.

To those who died without burial or cremation,
having fallen as bodies in the diaspora;
they chose death to forget sorrow and betray hope.
Death was a miracle for those who had lost life,
the tree on which a life without purpose hung;
those for whom living was the pinnacle of torture,
who sang of death as though it ushered a new life,
liberation, answering unasked questions.

To my people who went to the Second World War
without consulting the tripartite Gods of their land;
they left in a hurry and anger, perplexed to the bone,
because their Gods abandoned them.
When a man embarks on a distant and complex journey,
he shakes hands with his Gods before departure,
or share a libation for victory and safe return.
To my people, who wept before they became ashes

in Burma, Europe, Libya, and Egypt,
on the flaming pyres of stolen kingdoms,
to you, I say, you will return! You will come home.

To my people who died in African wildfires,
in the struggle for liberation from foreign foes,
for whom white was a symbol and a metaphor
for the liberation struggle, perfusion and infusion of blood;
for whom hope was a black uprising,
who slumped into the hole of despair of a migratory spirit;
who fell victim to a future that destroyed another,
by which venom took the place of living,
their dreams embalmed in the songs of today,
in the ballads that hang on our lips like tulips,
in the laughter echoing from treetops,
where they hang their God on a tree
for not gripping a sharp, sable spear
to pierce through the violence of their mockers.

To my people with braided hair and scalps,
who carried water pots on their heads with braids,
and whose fingers did not hide from the debris of kitchens,
who began to stink in the lethargy of drought,
or drowning or where no flowers paint the landscape,
aiming to halt the constant drain of their souls;
whose domestication was abused and misused
to prolong and propagate a servitude that fostered war.

How much is the cost of enslavement?
It's a life of seeking how to escape the rebellious streak,
which history has deposited on you like nuclear waste.
Now, we know what hate is, the holiness of the rainbow,
how needless the ugly require beauty to attain a destiny,
how they do not need the wind for their hair to dance;
the hurricane, the tornado, and the wild wind
can serve the same purpose where calm ends.
It's courageous and heroic to live on the other side of hope,
where there is a mirror to reflect how joy is alien to happiness,
how it is not relevant to be born in a country
to become its most loyal and ardent citizen.

Patriotism is a purchase and a cluster,
the knife unsheathed, the spear unbuckled,
where the gun rests cocked and breathing fire
to stop time from flowing like a running brook,
like air happily floating into yawning noses.
To my people who made history look like a canvas of blood,
I will make you live in defiance of the eclipse of time,
to challenge the change in time after
it has been woven into eternity.
If there is no sadness in tears, there can be no ending in death.

Jonathan Chibuike Ukah

To my people who live through the white light,
spreading its shadows across the diverse layers of darkness,
through the present as though it were the past,
through the spectrum where your souls weigh nothing
but the substance of a migratory swallow,
who live in the balcony of anger, hoping that it is bravery;
who, in memory of their noble acts, die,
in our remembrance of their heroism live eternally.

At My Father's Graveside

Hurrying to stand before you, Father,
I swallowed a whole dictionary of words,
stuffed with intricate sentences and phrases.
I can no longer express my mind's axis,
or why I decided to boycott your presence.
In my head, I acquired a universe of wisdom,
thinking I would build my mind's paradise,
where your tongue became a blurred memory.
I am ready to atone for my absence,
go on my knees to suck the dust.
I am prepared to eat up the lightning,
which your anger may provoke.
My eyes are blurred, and my heart is spinning
as my heart is thumping a million times.
I return and stand penitent before you,
a perplexed son, a fugitive of my town,
searching for words for a chapter of your eternity.

Over your desecrated grave,
I pour out my soul
like a river emptying into the ocean;
the silent sob of my sweated night,
which no words could echo.
I have returned a fragment,
a slice of your bone, a memorial,
lost in the words of my ancestors,

149

Jonathan Chibuike Ukah

filled with the storms of yesterday.
I am ashamed to see your grave,
littered with the grass of my absence;
wind-tossed leaves and twigs,
sterile dust in messy slurp,
mounds of a million termites,
and clusters of red anthills.
Before you, I swallowed sand,
I mouthed lumps of clay and mud.

As you always said, Father,
something mightier than the termite
has crept into the termite's hole;
and I wandered abroad
searching for something I never lost.
Though I wanted to discover how to return,
how to call you home again,
and transfer your grave to the sky.
I ended up swallowing galaxies,
clashing with universes,
wearing clouds in my need,
and scrubbing the moon.
Now, I have returned like a prodigal,
armed with an earthenware of earthworms,
willing to die in your presence
to live again.

Iya, The Magic Lady
Kathy Gregg

Ancestors, this world is
sick,

wicked,

demonic,

twisted.

I do not belong here, I never did.

This world sickens me.

This world torments me.

This world hates me.

This world loves and adores me.

How did I get trapped in this world of evil

disguised as humanity?

Was this a cruel joke

or am I dreaming

or am I just struggling to wake up?

Ancestors, please guide me

to the truth of my existence and reality;

Kathy Gregg

guide me to the truth of my creation
and let it be revealed.
My eyes are ready to see,
for delusion to be lifted,
for humanity has deceived me,
but you had it written in stone to remind me.
Out of the darkness
comes the light,
out of lies comes the truth.
To remain in darkness is to remain dead,
buried in the reality of your own mind.

Ancestors, bring me back to life
and revive my soul for it needs reviving,
and you hold the key to unlock the secrets
 that need to be told.
Arise ancestors,
arise for the return of my soul.
I come from the gypsies from a far away land—
Blue Hills to the Balkans
where my great grandmother and her ancestors
shed blood upon the land.
A lost culture; lost family,
she had to leave it behind
to erase her identity in hopes of a better life.

But was it worth it, Great Grandmother—
to give up your true identity and family?
Did you cry secret tears deep into the night?
I feel your pain; I see you in my dreams.
Long have I dreamed of dancing
as your spirit watches with great delight.
I, a woman of many races and many lands,
represent every continent
and every continent in me resides.

A lady of magic, mystery, and intrigue;
your gypsy ways passed on to me.
I will treasure the eleven years I knew you,
forever and ever and a day—
from India to the Balkans,
from your secret journey to the United States,
forever and ever, my mystery lady.
Though your American family did not honor you
the way you deserved,
I shall honor you with this poem,
which you well deserve, my Magic Lady.

Kathy Gregg

JUSTICE
The Cry of the Land

Section 7

Art as Social Justice
Carmen dela Cruz

A witness to what is often ignored,
a voice for the marginalized that ignites movements,
it serves to soothe the wounds repeatedly opened, and re-injured,
to speak with a pen, a quill, a paintbrush,
in strokes of movement with hands and legs,
stomping to the beat of a drum,
drumming,
drumming,
drumming notes from the ancestors,
passed on and transformed to drums,
rapping over the same beat,
but drumming,
drumming,
with fingers running over keyboards,

a message that cannot be done with the parting of lips,

if not in song,

wrapped in verse,

cyphered,

and scribed in ink,

to utter words to those that have othered us,

made us feel unseen,

marred, like a false note,

an unrhymed, off beat melody,

but our note is just the right note,

just the right unique tempo,

our story need not fit carefully into a loop of the system;

Black against a white line,

we color outside,

dance outside to our own beats,

and our pens sing what we cannot.

Circuitous Revolution

Ryan Files

The revolution will not be televised
The revolution will not be televised
It has instead been cut
into a 30-second TikTok video for your consumption
The revolution's OnlyFans will give you liberation
for a monthly payment of 19.69
Nice...
Reddit renaissance for '20
"April Rain Song" respite puffing cares away
in the early spring storm
"Give me liberty or give me death!"
sayeth the slave owner Henry
Did he have a hammer in his hand?
Isn't it ironic, don't you think?
Spotify plays white girl jams
as the viola echoes a single note

Liuzzo freedom rides no more for equality
but Lizzo echoes, "Good as Hell" from the Echo Dot
Stop, the clock spots another victim
Oh dear, I shall be too late!
Silly rabbit, the glock popped one
hit wonders on my Instagram feed
Is it Floyd or is it Diallo?
Or is it Jimmie Lee or maybe Evers?
I can never get it right
Too many Black squares to cover the blood in the streets
Or hands
Or flags
Post flagged on X
At least Band-Aids match my skin color
and syrup and rice aren't racist anymore
Went to the Wells of People's Grocery
Always low prices
Discounts that'll kill
I've Till'd the soil while whistling a tune
Streamed Disney Plus to watch a cartoon
This movie may have material one finds offensive
Would you like to skip this ad?

Ignore all isn't an option on this screen
So, I put a blindfold over my eyes and called it justice
I searched to find *Song of the South*
but it felt more like a Lost Cause
Br'er rabbit said, it's about time
to put on my Mickey Mouse minstrel gloves
Come inside; it's fun inside!
I'm stuck in this br'er patch
Sew it shut with my hand over my mouth
Don't mention it
Or is it a hand over a heart?
The Truth is in the social
We had the perfect start
But couldn't finish a race
that chained people to the start line
Do you have the time
on when the revolution starts?

Not About the Color of Our Skin

Lucas Rivera

This is not about the color of our skin.
It is about the internal effects
superior complexes have on a people.
It is about strolling dark streets,
checking your six every six seconds.
It is about not being able to put our hoodies on
when our heads are cold.

It is about the loneliness
entrapped in our consciousness,
waiting for hope to ring.
It is about the ringing in our ears
after loud bangs take our brothers,
sisters, fathers, mothers.
It is about burying our children
before they hit puberty.
It is about going through metal detectors
only to see daddy's innocence
lost in the pupil of his eyes.

Lucas Rivera

It is about black lives,
black souls,
black love you can't confine.

It is about the way you look at me
and the way I look at you.
It is about the fear that overcomes our skin
when the police pull up behind us,
instigating us to make a mistake.
It is about high blood pressure,
drug use, and nightmares–
            someday we may go back to that time.
It is about the ways that you remember
and remind us to stay in our place.

Then,
It is about our stance that remains proud,
a heart that can't be bound.
It is about the way we rise
and the ways you continue to push us down.
It is about generational trauma
and a voice in our souls that SCREAMS "¡NO MÁS!"

It is not about the color of our skin,
But it *is* about the million reasons
our skin continues to be a victim of...

Questions for the State of Iowa
Aanika Pfister

Dear Iowa,
　　Why do you think you were

voted the ugliest state in the nation?

Farmers say you are beautiful.

Your fields flow with stalks of gold

for them. 4.73 a bushel. For them.

Your roads fork for the McDonald's for them

The HyVee for them; you've given them

everything they need! Soybeans and

teeny tiny towns to raise

White children in.

So, why do you think you were voted

the ugliest state in the nation?

Aanika Pfister

Dear Iowa,
How did you survive their I-235
which split you in half
which steam-piled your neighborhoods
your prairies, your butterflies, your bees
and Center Street, Des Moines—original
Black Haven
where jazz bands fanned
out from The Sepia Club
Pink gin and performances in greyscale
attended by your people?

The Black and Indigenous
forced to move like rats.
One red line splitting you through for
Des Moines' coronary bypass
I pass by it daily.
Dear Iowa,
People used to live there.

Dear Iowa,
Did you know your soil is coveted?
If you cover it in seeds—
red cabbage, and spinach,
green peppers, and rose, and
it grows like nowhere else?
They call it Black Gold.

Dear Iowa,
Did you know there are black people still living
in your boundaries and attending your
universities, working because
they believe in something you can give?
I call them Black Gold.

Dear Iowa,
Did you know you hold in your arms
the worst city in America
to be black?
Waterloo—
where the citizens suffer from
constant carcinogens
and the land around them is bowed
from someone else's crops?
4.73 a bushel. The price of a Starbucks latte
for rot and degradation.
Why do you think you were voted
the ugliest state in the nation?
Dear Iowa,
I moved here expecting "fields of opportunities,"
cheap degrees, and close-knit communities,
and instead, I've gotten your pavement,
your disrespect, your congress.

Aanika Pfister

Dear Iowa,
Home of the wild rose,
of some of the nicest folks
of occasional oxbow, of quiet, and of rain.
Your gold doesn't grow in fields.
We grow in the streets.
You: First free state in the purchase.
You: First to desegregate schools.
You: ugliest state in the nation
whose worth has been measured only in bushels
in land that is changed
and times that are gone.

Dear Iowa,
We know you are beautiful
but Black Gold isn't renewable.
Show us all of your love
or lose us.

To the Black Angels
Aanika Pfister

*H*old on, *just a little while longer;*
Everything will be alright.

Black folks sing that song
in a church filled up with White angels.
Bows perched, cheeks plump,
perfect babies;
godly apparitions
whose honor it is to be Jesus's adornments.

Black girl is awestruck by the angels.
She thinks they're adorable,
and she hopes to find them
wherever Jesus hangs in Heaven
if she gets there.

So, she tries to get A's in school.
She is smart, but not nearly like
Ashley Penner,
who's got confidence like
her heavenly passport's already been stamped in gold.
She wears those nice leggings, and
she drinks Starbucks every morning, and
she like—has that like—nice way of talking—
that like—makes her seem like—she's bound to be popular.
And what is a Black girl bound to be?
She is no Ashley Penner, so she gets B's.

In history, she reads about the greats;
Edison, Jefferson, Washington.
She thinks she wants to be a statue outside—
immortalized—
like those White dudes who
changed history or changed America.
But there is nothing for her here.
She is not White-cast, statuette material,
and she is not pastel pink angel material either.

She realizes this on Instagram.
Hands shaking she sees
White beauty and nothing else.

She sees thin ladies and tight sweaters,
and white mannequins,
and sassy Black best friends.
Suddenly, Statue outside is an
unattainably White heavenly light,
a scalding light,
a godly apparition reminding—
Yes, Jesus was a White man.
But Abe Lincoln was too
and didn't he set you free?
It preaches
Emancipation Proclamation,
a moment of contemplation.
Forget Reconstruction
and stand for your nation.
We love you, now.

And it speaks nothing of Black angels.
She sings,

Hold on,
Just a little while longer;
Everything will be alright.

Aanika Pfister

Until it's not.
Until she feels like an alien in her own skin.
Until it's not.
Until she starts to seek out her history
in tomes, not in statues—in poetry.

Until she solves dark mysteries and starts
seeing every speck of dust as an unwritten ancestor,
every drop from the water fountain,
a grandmama who threw herself to sea
and sunk.
Until she Sojourns and finds her Truth—

That Black angels aren't in stained glass.
And Black suffering isn't in school books.
But Black angels live!
And hell yeah—they hang with Jesus up in heaven
with the White ones!
But most of them breed in the city
and sit
in the lips of Eartha Kitt,
bathe in Lupita Nyong'o's skin;
sink into Black folks' bones and solidify into a
heavenly gold.

Black girl is awestruck by the angels.
They have painted the sky black every night
in celebration of us.
And every Sunday, they've filled up the churches,
filed into the seats or drifted into the air and sang,

Everything will be alright!

Purple Poet Tree
Karen Lynette Jones

Deeper Than

Slavery is not the end of atrocities
suffered by minority communities.
The everyday systematic sway
off bricks piled against you
like a wall of pain
so many bricks
the millions murdered for simply being
who they were born to be
black brown red.
But of these
I speak of what I know firsthand –
the professional personal political assassination
of the collective black character, so deep,
it is astonishingly ingrained and denied to be a thing.

Karen Lynette Jones

For instance, because there was a black president
in this racist country
people say there you have equality
nope
a system built on the back of blacks
that promotes hate of anything black.
Saving a few teachers pets
does not save the souls of those
still being oppressed stressed and put to death.
Schools are a battleground as well,
we are not even teaching the truth freely.
Jim Crow is alive and well,
look it up.

The systems of government, used and abused,
keep people from getting the American Dream
the poor displaced and disgraced
taxed to the max
while the rich enjoy perks
less tax relax
when I walk in a store I am sized up and categorized
followed by security.
I may get service,
but only if I look affluent enough.
sometimes not even then.
Depends of the store,
depends of the area.

When my brother walks down the street,
do you clutch your purse?
No really.
if he doesn't style himself just so,
is he perceived as less than?
When he goes to the bank for a loan,
how often will he be denied
or unfairly penalized?

It's deeper than slavery
we are still here suffering despite being
called Americans,
we are treated
not even as well as foreigners
who seek asylum.

Where is *that* for the brown red black people?
It's not being able to fairly compete for jobs
when corporate snobs ask for degrees and experience
but how do you get one before the other.

When you don't qualify for loans
or go in so much debt for college
that the dream is deferred.
Or, you get the job, but the pay
is poor because you can't afford the degree.
Never mind you are doing the job perfectly,
you must get multiple jobs to eat.

Karen Lynette Jones

I'm so sick of saying
that marginalized systematic racism
in America goes far beyond
than what happened then
it is what is happening now, today.
And, by the looks of it, its all the future holds
as the systems of old have not been replaced!

Black and Blue

You never ask
my race my face
tell a solid story or two
of a possible relationship to ancestors.
an old African truth

You mistake my hair for weave
or some other mystery;
it kinks and curls down my back
it waves, water prompting,
they all asked you got Indian in you?
Why do I have to be anything other than black and beautiful?

Of course my ancestors were raped
my blues come from all kinds of hate
suffered by my chocolate race
from men to women to babes
no one dares say
my black is blue in all its cool

Images of singing blinging truths
it's beauty like blue eyes in brown cousins
it's duty like blue cries and night lovin'

Karen Lynette Jones

You never say you see a queen in me
a queen who survives despite defeat
of broken dreams
of broken body
strong enough to love and still will piece
my black is blue of an unknown tribe

Look beyond my hips and their lips that lie
don't you mind condemning Hitlers kind,
the KKK and police are fine?
My black is blue like a deep sea
the universe weaved me
to bring forth life in every shade
you can't deny me
as you can't wash off your face
and wash DNA away

Move Mountains

Even when there's snow on the roof
I will have fire in the chimney
I will keep a warm hopeful heart
and a strong steady mind
determined, despite my flaws,
to win it all
life love liberty

My ancestors lived
                    died in chains
in hopes that I may live
                    die free
their tears salted the earth
as they walked with bloody feet
no shoes but splendid souls
only the strongest survived
that I may live so

I can move mountains
learning that which can't be taught
acquiring assets that can't be bought
I am the eagle that flies the highest
when my enemy stoops the lowest
to reach my destination
I can move mountains for others

Karen Lynette Jones

that only seem a pebble to me
for my mind has broken it up
into many rocks
defeated any negative thinking
linking mind over matter
I will use
my gifts my wits my back my tits
all my personal asset
grab it and run with it

For my days are numbered
not by fear of death
but aware
I must clear the path
–just as ancestors have–
I stand on raw shoulders
and I am too a stepping stone
when I move this mountain
I don't do so alone

Lisa's Love Jones

She is another man's property
forbidden perhaps to pose for such an artist
a mirage slow smile on her face
some see smirk,
somber sliver sly, seduction
sandy shadows shape her presence
did you see, in her encore eyes,
dreams deferred/decorated/delivered
in a decidedly departed deja vu?

Hidden in brave denial
the remainder of her doting smile
traced/enhanced/romanced by his hands
attentive artistry –bleak bronze hues–
captures light behind enchanting eyes

Maybe she carries a child
painted in her womb by her lovers brush
swelling hearts baptizing minds
as the only work of art she will treasure
for it is so very personal
love lights Mona Lisa's darkest daze
painted passion lives in an impression
a hinting a smile
least the secret be told too loud

Karen Lynette Jones

Learning to Persevere

Learning to play piano again
like a toddler learning how to walk
my fingers fumble
like a sin a wrong note shrills in the air

The note hangs
choking melodies
my brain aspires to create

Oh, how I miss my youthful fingertips
once nimble flexible, accurate
now nerve damage curves their abilities

Gasp, I must ignore reading music
but rather adore grasping sound by ear
frustrated but of good cheer
for if a famed musician can not see
yet plays beautifully I must not be weak
if a musician turns deaf
still has the skill to work treble clef
I too must persevere and do well
the ancestors demand this of me

RESILIENCE

Past and Present

Section 8

Resistance, Resilience, and Resurrection
Ade Anita Johnson

Extra, Extra

Extra, extra read all about it
there's a reckoning coming for you
Extra, extra look at the view
what we don't recognize will break us in two.

Breaking news interrupts your feed
Conflicts rising like ravenous weeds
Suffocating under the weight of the words we say
We write down history with red ink
Lies to divide, not just my legacy
But all the intricate parts of we.

Ade Anita Johnson

Blood-stained history gives birth to fresh
Ways of leaving our nation's hands unclean
What you see cannot be unseen
Your own two eyes do not deceive
We scream beneath the heavy headlines
wrapped in bullet casings.

What's black, white, and read all over
With headlines that read *Blue Lives Matter*
Even as Black lives shatter under another knee
Blood runs in the street
Family screams silently, while judges set another killer free
Thought blue was the color of serenity, but
Ain't nobody came yet to keep the peace.

Extra, extra read all about it
this nation still celebrates slavery
Extra, extra read all about it
southern tree blood covers cold concrete.

Hiding behind hospitality, we still celebrate slavery
With all its vicious brutality
Statues honoring the brutal, violent, weak
Leaders of an insurgency plotting to split the country
Take out democracy—just to keep owning Black bodies
In print, email, TV, movies, podcast, or just
The word on the street.

I pick up your newspaper, but I'm still running
Between black and white lines
My soul slipping from Black body to Black body
To Black minds surviving for centuries on the vine.

You think 400 years got us beat?
Naw, we got an unbroken chain of ancestral heartbeats
Still drumming
Hands bleeding, feet pounding, sweat beads breaking up
the compacted earth mound
You have been trampling down
to deaden the sound of triumphant rebound.

Yea, we bleed, we scream, suffocated under your pointed knees
Broken we may seem, but our blood is dripping
into the streams of your children's dreams
You can kill a body
but not a haunting
It doesn't matter what you believe
When an army of spirits intercedes
The headlines will read...

Extra, extra read all about it
there's a reckoning coming for you.

Ade Anita Johnson

The Greens Speak

I met these three on the way to the farmer's market
community.
A trio of greens
that spoke to me, led me to consider their history.
Instead of choosing one.
they insisted I grab all three.
Greens speak, speaking greens, the soil of our dreams.
They were sassy, fine, wise, and funny,
urging me to see their resilient beauty.

The fine one stepped up to me,
confident and speaking freely,
"I am peppery and spicy. I curl beautifully,
my textured flowers under feet, a true culinary treat."
Greens speak, speaking greens see.
"My beauty comes in red, purple, and shades of green.
I bring sustenance strong,
I carry the weight of history in my leaves.
Child, you wouldn't believe what I've seen.
I breathe in sunlight and extract water from earth's feet.
I believe in sturdy possibilities of plenty."

Greens speak, tell truth about things.
Speaking greens blend and soften.
"In solidarity with onions, garlic and salty meat,
I shine as the curly beauty;

holding memories of centuries
grown to provide nutrients seen and unseen
from magnesium to calcium to the forgotten Vitamin K,
I am the mustard green,
enriching the body, soothing the soul today,
mustering a path for a healing."

The wise one pushed Mustard aside to speak,
his tone serious, confident, and complete.
"She may be cute and curly, but
I bring the tough spine of a warrior leaf—
not to be messed with.
I can endure brutal and toxic energies.
Dark green with a thick, light spine;
I play well with mustard and turnip leaves,
but I'm as solid as a tree.
Bitter at times, but persistently firm through hours of
chopping, braising, simmering, boiling—
with proper handling, I am a joy to eat.
A hearty leaf, I fill bellies all through this land,
around the globe and across the sea.
Folks holler for me, 'Y'all got any collards?' That's me!
My leaf is wide and stiff. Try me raw,
but simmer me long with spices and love.
Add some hot sauce, put your foot in me, and you'll see
 I'll make you wanna slap your grandmama... gently."

Ade Anita Johnson

Greens speak, speaking greens of legacy.
The funny green was the last to speak,
hopping out in front of me.
Determined to go home in my basket too;
she shared her piece brilliantly
"Mustards and Collards believe they are superior,
top of the green royalty,
but I'm here to tell you, when I turn up,
I put the rest to shame. I play no games.
Add me to the pot to pepper things up.
I might be a bit prickly to touch;
I'm a long, lean healing machine
that can reduce your swelling,
keep your heart beating, even attack the cancer beast.
I may be last to speak, but eat some turnip greens,
my healing leaves will make you sing,
bring any illness to its knees.
I'm more than just a turnip weed,
I'm a magnificent green beauty."

Greens speak, create possibility.
Speaking greens nurture my people's dreams
when all had spoke,
I looked around to see no one else had been listening.
I heard my ancestors rattling off recipes.
It was an easy choice for me to gather up all three.
Although slapping my grandmama,
I'm quite sure is not a wise choice for you or me.

Buried Bodies (Await Resurrection)

My timid steps speak in earth shattering creaks,
as I move closer into the cobwebbed, locked down crypt
lying dormant,
covered in blood red ivy
growing like fungus over dying bodies.
I left in a rush from the crush of childhood imagining,
severed heads of blooming worlds planted in the core of me.

No time to gather the things I held holy,
 the carnage of mind, body and soul. It was an energy.
The humans protecting me,
they couldn't see
the father above knows they do not mean
        to wield murderous axes
        so violently at the growing child in me.
The world shoots arrows blindly, a gut reaction to the pain
        they buried next to me in rows and rows
        of gravestones,
        drenched in treachery, greed, hypocrisy—
        a painful legacy.
        The angels left without numbing me.

    The uncovering would be my destiny.
Steamy stench rises up in me, will not let me be.
So, I run back to the scene of the tragedy,
brace myself to release.
Speak out loud to all who lay deaf, dumb, blind, and dying.
Speak of the pain affecting we.

Ade Anita Johnson

Scream like a brilliant Black banshee
warning of the decaying death I see.
Run ravenously;
ripping Band-aids off to blood-curdling screams,
even the dead bleed when they hear me.
Feel cat claw sting of razor,
cutting the strong from the weak,
exposing the infected wounds to air,
emotional, physical, mental, spiritual healing—
I know where your body of longing lays in unrest.
I know where your body of self-hate
sweats in the melting heat beneath the crematory.
I know where your body of creativity lies,
        a spirit, crazy walking the midnight graveyards
        in heavy mist babbling.
I know where your body of love lies buried
        beneath the decaying flesh of those weighted bodies
        that just crushed thee rather than lift your heart up to beat,
        that love body never dies, it just bleeds incessantly
        leaking into the soul and
        carried into the next life, weeping for a love to hold.
I know where your bodies are buried, your silent sex tragedies,
        limp emotional grip
        barren scratchy pleas for nonexistent intimacy,
        your childhood boogie man bullies still chasing you
        into middle-age, blooded and
        bruised, reaching for phantom victories,

your lonely cries to a God
you believe ain't listening,
    generational acid burn, searing your fresh skin
    randomly.
I know where your bodies are buried,
and I've wrapped myself
    in the white fire of spiritual warfare,
    laced up with the marching, walking dead
    dancing to victory
    in some Dia de los Muertos parade party.
Stepped fiercely into the rotting crypt,
they thought was hid from me.
I know where the bodies are dead, and
I am setting bones ablaze,
releasing our hearts, we need to face the fear.
Loud
deafening beats to drum past the silence,
walk amongst the dead, clear.

Armored in the line of elevated spirits lifting me.
Yea, though I walk through the valley
of the shadow of death and buried bodies,
I exhume light-filled beautiful dreams,
christening inhaling, my belly growing
amongst the walking dead, I am able to breathe.

Ade Anita Johnson

Go back to the covered graves of your history.
Go back, do not wait!
Your fate's water rises and stirs.
Tsunamis rarely leave you standing,
but they can break down ancient gates.
Break open the crypt doors.
Strip your mummies down to the core.
Go find your decaying bodies,
fearlessly fight your shadowed fear;
stand victorious and come walk with me.
Let the sweet and salt waters of your destiny
leave you clean,
        your path pristine,
                Your resilient resurrection is near.

Sibling Sobriety

Trish Broome

Trauma.
Grief.
Addiction.
We didn't have it way back when.
Naive and young.
Having fun.
Watching dad drink in the den.
He'd start to grin
then tip it in.
Scary movies, up 'til ten.
We'd get a hug, then go to sleep.
He'd repeat again.

Trish Broome

When he left, it stayed inside.

Slowly crept into our lives.

It kept us connected.

I often cried.

Got worse when he died.

I wanted it to stop.

Trauma.

Grief.

Addiction.

All the shit we got from pop.

It got worse and multiplied.

You, all alone, and me with a kid.

Struggling to live

and love

like we once did.

Smile. Grin. Tip it in.

Sadness erased for only a minute.

Separate lives, yet we went through

this hell together, me and you.

We're black and blue.

"Life is a wheel of fortune and it's my turn to spin it."

That's what Tupac said. So, let's win it—

Together.

Persistence

Jonathan Chibuike Ukah

When it rains
and drowns the insects;
when the flood rises like a long wall,
build a house inside the river
and let its roofs be the water
surging as waves into your body.
Doors and windows are but the tributaries
through which the river empties itself
inside the ocean;
you must see the sun shining,
though it hides behind the clouds.
You must see it clearly,
dancing in the middle of the sky,
waving with ten fingers.

Jonathan Chibuike Ukah

When it is dark,
you must see the light
piercing in every corner, every time,
changing night to day,
black to white, green to yellow,
creating shadows where there are none
showing you the way forward.
You must learn to build a house,
putting one block after the other,
one zinc after the other,
one wood after the other,
one iron after the other
until they reach the roof.

And when the road closes,
it must be opened;
there is no closure without aperture,
without the key to unlock the door,
without a secret door that only you can see,
a side road leading you to the goal.

The day is long that is short,
when it is not enough to end our duty,
but enough for the rest we deserve.
We can make boredom go away,
tedium to be a joyous celebration.
We can rejoice in the loneliness

that arrives with so much multitude.
And if sadness looms like a train,
let the flowers of laughter,
happiness and peace await it
at the station where it must halt,
refuel, and perhaps change drivers.
The onward departure is the safest arrival,
and there will be a cascading down of hope.

If obstacles litter your path like dry leaves,
It's thanksgiving season.
The harvest will be immense;
there shall be new fruits,
new seeds, and fresh vegetables,
which birds and goats can share
in a new world created by hindrances.

When there is drought,
there will be rivers and seas
surrounding every desert.
Oceans will abound in the sky like points of light,
spots of oases decorate the earth like swirling lights.
You will draw patterns on the ground,
in labyrinth like the contours of a Zebra,
out of which funnels of clear water emerge.

With no apologies.

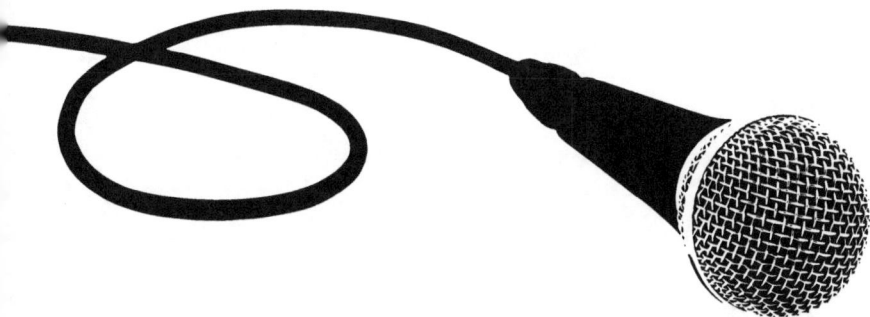

www.ingramcontent.com/pod-product-compliance
Lightning Source LLC
LaVergne TN
LVHW051231080426
835513LV00016B/1521